The complete book of
MIXED DRINKS

R&R PUBLICATIONS MARKETING PTY LTD

Published by:
R&R Publications Marketing Pty. Ltd
12 Edward Street, Brunswick, Victoria 3056, Australia
Australia-wide toll-free 1 800 063 296
E-mail: info@randrpublications.com.au
Web: www.randrpublications.com.au

Publisher: Richard Carroll
Mixed Drinks Research: Jon Carroll
Creative Director: Paul Sims
Project Manager: Anthony Carroll
Photography: Warren Webb
Presentation: Jon Carroll
Photography Assistance: Samantha Carroll

The National Library of Australia
Cataloguing-in-Publication Data
The complete book of mixed drinks.
Includes index.
ISBN: 0 681 37743 7

1. Cocktails. 2. Beverages. 3. Alcoholic beverages.

Printed: May 1994, 1996, 1997, 1999, 2001, 2002, 2003
This edition printed November 2005

Computer Typeset in ITC Eras and Palatino
Printed in Singapore

Table of Contents

METHODS OF MIXING COCKTAILS

The four methods below are the most common processes of mixing cocktails:-

1. Shake   **2.** Stir
3. Build   **4.** Blend

1. SHAKE: To shake is to mix a cocktail by shaking it in a cocktail shaker by hand. First, fill the glass part of the shaker three quarters full with ice, then pour the ingredients on top of the ice. Less expensive ingredients are more frequently poured before the deluxe ingredients. Pour the contents of the glass into the metal part of the shaker and shake vigorously for ten to fifteen seconds. Remove the glass section and using a Hawthorn strainer, strain contents into the cocktail glass. Shaking ingredients that do not mix easily with spirits is easy and practical (juices, egg whites, cream and sugar syrups).

Most shakers have two or three parts. In a busy bar, the cap is often temporarily misplaced. If this happens, a coaster or the inside palm of your hand is quite effective. American shakers are best.

To sample the cocktail before serving to the customer, pour a small amount into the shaker cap and using a straw check the taste.

2. STIR: To stir a cocktail is to mix the ingredients by stirring them with ice in a mixing glass and then straining them into a chilled cocktail glass. Short circular twirls are most preferred. (NB. The glass part of the American shaker will do well for this.) Spirits, liqueurs and vermouths that blend easily together are mixed by this method.

3. BUILD: To build a cocktail is to mix the ingredients in the glass in which the cocktail is to be served, floating one on top of the other. Hi-Ball, long fruit juice and carbonated mixed cocktails are typically built using this technique. Where possible a swizzle stick should be put into the drink to mix the ingredients after being presented to the customer. Long straws are excellent substitutes when swizzle sticks are unavailable.

4. BLEND: To blend a cocktail is to mix the ingredients using an electric blender/mixer. It is recommended to add the fruit (fresh or tinned) first. Slicing small pieces gives a smoother texture than if you add the whole fruit. Next, pour the alcohol. Ice should always be added last. This order ensures that the fruit is blended freely with the alcoholic ingredients allowing the ice to gradually mix into the food and beverage, chilling the flavour. Ideally, the blender should be on for at least 20 seconds. Following this procedure will prevent ice and fruit lumps that then need to be strained.

If the blender starts to rattle and hum, ice may be obstructing the blades from spinning. Always check that the blender is clean before you start. Angostura Bitters is ammonia based which is suitable for cleaning. Fill 4 to 5 shakes with hot water, rinse and then wipe clean.

TECHNIQUES IN MAKING COCKTAILS

1. SHAKE AND POUR: After shaking the cocktail, pour the contents straight into the glass. When pouring into Hi-Ball glasses and sometimes old fashioned glasses the ice cubes are included. This eliminates straining.

2. SHAKE AND STRAIN: Using a Hawthorn strainer (or knife) this technique prevents the ice going into the glass. Straining protects the cocktail ensuring melted ice won't dilute the flavour and mixture.

3. FLOAT INGREDIENTS: Hold the spoon right way up and rest it with the lip slightly above the level of the last layer. Fill spoon gently and the contents will flow smoothly from all around the rim. Use the back of the spoons dish only if you are experienced.

4. FROSTING (sugar and salt rims): This technique is used to coat the rim of the glass with either salt or sugar. First, rub lemon/orange slice juice all the way around only the glass rim. Next, holding the glass by the stem upside down, rest on a plate containing salt or sugar and turn slightly so that it adheres to the glass. Pressing the glass too deeply into the salt or sugar often results in chunks sticking to the glass. A lemon slice is used for salt and an orange slice is used for sugar.

To achieve colour affects, put a small amount of grenadine or coloured liqueur in a plate and coat the rim of the glass, then gently place in the sugar. The grenadine absorbs the sugar and turns it pink. This is much easier than mixing grenadine with sugar and then trying to get it to stick to the glass.

HELPFUL HINTS

Cocktail mixing is an art which is expressed in the preparation and presentation of the cocktail.

HOW TO MAKE A BRANDY ALEXANDER CROSS

Take two short straws and, with a sharp knife, slice one of the straws half way through in the middle and wedge the other uncut straw into the cut straw to create a cross.

STORING FRUIT JUICES

Take a 750ml bottle and soak it in hot water to remove the label and sterilise the alcohol. The glass has excellent appeal and you'll find it easier to pour the correct measurement with an attached nip pourer.

SUGAR SYRUP RECIPE

Fill a cup or bowl (depending on how much you want to make) with white sugar, top it up with boiling water until the receptacle is just about full and keep stirring until the sugar is fully dissolved. Refrigerate when not in use. Putting a teaspoon of sugar into a cocktail is being lazy, it does not do the job properly as the sugar dissolves.

JUICE TIPS

Never leave juices, Coconut Cream or other ingredients in cans. Pour them into clean bottles, cap and refrigerate them. All recipes in this book have been tested with Berri fruit juices.

ICE

Ice is probably the most important part of cocktails. It is used in nearly all cocktails. Consequently ice must be clean and fresh at all times.

The small squared cubes and flat chips of ice are superior for chilling and mixing cocktails. Ice cubes with holes are inefficient. Wet ice, ice scraps and broken ice should only be used in blenders.

CRUSHED ICE

Take the required amount of ice and fold into a clean linen cloth. Although uncivilised, the most effective method is to smash it against the bar floor. Shattering with a bottle may break the bottle. Certain retailers sell portable ice crushers. Alternatively a blender may be used. Half fill with ice and then pour water into the blender until it reaches the level of the ice. Blend for about 30 seconds, strain out the water and you have perfectly crushed ice. Always try and use a metal scoop to collect the ice from the ice tray.

Never pick up the ice with your hands. This is unhygienic. Shovelling the glass into the ice tray to gather ice can also cause breakages and hence should be avoided where possible.

It is important that the ice tray is cleaned each day. As ice is colourless and odourless, many people assume wrongly it is always clean. Taking a cloth soaked in hot water, wipe the inside of the bucket warm. The blenders used for all of our bar requirements are Moulinex blenders with glass bowls. We have found these blenders to be of exceptional quality.

GLASSES

Cordial (Embassy):	30mL	Fancy Hi-Ball Glass:	220mL, 350mL, 470mL
Cordial (Lexington):	37mL	Hurricane Glass:	230mL, 440mL, 650mL
Tall Dutch Cordial:	45mL	Irish Coffee Glass:	250mL
Whisky Shot:	45mL	Margarita Glass:	260mL
Martini Glass:	90mL	Hi-Ball Glass:	270mL, 285mL, 330mL
Cocktail Glass:	90mL, 140mL	Footed Hi-Ball Glass:	270mL, 300mL
Champagne Saucer:	140mL	Salud Grande Glass:	290mL
Champagne Flute:	140mL, 180mL	Fiesta Grande Glass:	350mL, 490mL
Wine Goblet:	140mL, 190mL	Poco Grande Glass:	380mL
Old Fashioned Spirit:	185mL, 210mL, 290mL	Brandy Balloon:	650mL
Fancy Cocktail:	210mL, 300mL		

A proven method to cleaning glasses is to hold each glass individually over a bucket of boiling water until the glass becomes steamy and then with a clean linen cloth rub in a circular way to ensure the glass is polished for the next serve

Cocktails can be poured into any glass but the better the glass the better the appearance of the cocktail.

One basic rule should apply and that is, use no coloured glasses as they spoil the appearance of cocktails. All glasses have been designed for a specific task, e.g.,

1. Hi-Ball glasses for long cool refreshing drinks.
2. Cocktail glasses for short sharp, or stronger drinks.
3. Champagne saucers for creamy after-dinner style drinks, etc.,

The stem of the glass has been designed so you may hold it whilst polishing, leaving the bowl free of marks and germs so that you may enjoy your drink. All cocktail glasses should be kept in a refrigerator or filled with ice while you are preparing the cocktails in order to chill the glass. An appealing affect on a 90ml cocktail glass can be achieved by running the glass under cold water and then placing it in the freezer.

GARNISHES AND JUICES

Banana	Onions
Celery	Oranges
Cucumber	Pineapple
Lemons	Red Maraschino Cherries
Limes	Rockmelon
Mint leaves	Strawberries
Olives	Canned fruit
Celery salt	Nutmeg
Chocolate flake	Pepper, Salt
Cinnamon	Tomato
Fresh eggs	Sugar and sugar cubes
Fresh single cream	Tabasco sauce
Fresh milk	Worcestershire sauce
Apple	Orange and Mango
Carbonated waters	Pineapple
Coconut Cream	Sugar syrup
Lemon – pure	Canned nectars
Orange	Canned pulps
Jelly Babies	Crushed Pineapple
Almonds	Blueberries
Apricot Conserve	Red Cocktail Onions
Vanilla Ice Cream	Flowers (assorted)

Simplicity is the most important fact to keep in mind when garnishing cocktails. Do not overdo the garnish; make it striking, but if you can't get near the cocktail to drink it then you have failed. Most world champion cocktails just have a lemon slice, or a single red cherry.

Tall refreshing Hi-Balls tend to have more garnish as the glass is larger. A swizzle stick should be served nearly always in long cocktails. Straws are always served for a lady, but optional for a man.

Plastic animals, umbrellas, fans and a whole variety of novelty goods are now available to garnish with, and they add a lot of fun to the drink.

ALCOHOL RECOMMENDED FOR A COCKTAIL BAR

Spirits

Ouzo	Scotch
Bourbon	Southern Comfort
Brandy	Tennessee Whiskey
Campari	Tequila
Canadian Club	Vandermint
Gin	Vodka
Malibu	
Pernod	
Rum	

Liqueurs

Advocaat	Frangelico
Amaretto	Galliano
Bailey's Irish Cream	Grand Marnier
Banana	Kahlúa
Benedictine	Kirsch
Blue Curacao	Kirsch
Cassis	Mango
Chartreuse – Green & Yellow	Melon
Cherry Advocaat	Orange
Cherry Brandy	Peach
Clayton's Tonic (Non-alcoholic)	Pimm's
Coconut	Sambuca – Clear
Cointreau	Sambuca – Black
Creme de cafe	Strawberry
Creme de Menthe Green	Triple Sec
Dark Creme de Cacao	
Drambuie	

Vermouth

Cinzano Bianco Vermouth	Martini Bianco Vermouth
Cinzano Dry Vermouth	Martini Dry Vermouth
Cinzano Rosso Vermouth	Martini Rosso Vermouth

ESSENTIAL EQUIPMENT FOR A COCKTAIL BAR

Cocktail shaker	Waiter's friend corkscrew
Hawthorn Strainer	Bottle openers
Mixing glass	Ice scoop
Spoon with muddler	Ice bucket
Moulinex Electric blender	Free pourers
Knife, cutting board	Swizzle sticks, straws
Measures (jiggers)	Coasters and napkins
Can opener	Scooper spoon (long teaspoon)
Hand cloths for cleaning glasses	

DESCRIPTION OF LIQUEURS AND SPIRITS

Advocaat: A combination of fresh egg whites, yolks, sugar, brandy, vanilla and spirit. Limited shelf life, Recommend shelf life 12-15 months from manufacture.

Amaretto: A rich subtle liqueur with a unique almond flavour.

Angostura Bitters: An essential part of any bar or kitchen. A unique additive whose origins date back to 1824. A mysterious blend of natural herbs and spices, both a seasoning and flavouring agent, in both sweet and savoury dishes and drinks. Ideal for dieters as it is low in sodium and calories.

Baileys Irish Cream: The largest selling liqueur in the world.

slt is a blend of Irish Whiskey, softened by Irish Cream and other flavourings. It is a natural product.

Banana: Fresh ripe bananas are the perfect base for the definitive daiquiri and a host of other exciting fruit cocktails.

Benedictine: A perfect end to a perfect meal. Serve straight, with ice, soda, or as part of a favourite cocktail.

Bourbon – Has a smooth, deep, easy flavour.

Brandy – Smooth and mild spirit, is considered a very smooth and palatable, ideal for mixing.

Campari: A drink for many occasions, both as a long or short drink, or as a key ingredient in many fashionable cocktails.

Cassis: Deep, rich purple promises and delivers a regal and robust flavour and aroma. Cassis lends itself to neat drinking or an endless array of delicious sauces and desserts.

Chartreuse: A liqueur available in either yellow or green colour. Made by the monks of the Carthusian order. The only world famous liqueur still made by monks.

Cherry Advocaat: Same as Advocaat, plus natural cherry flavours and colour is added.

Cherry Brandy: Is made from concentrated, morello cherry juice. Small quantity of bitter almonds and vanilla is added to make it more enjoyable as a neat drink before or after dinner. Excellent for mixers, topping, ice cream, fruit salads, pancakes, etc.

Coconut: A smooth liqueur, composed of exotic coconut, heightened with light-bodied white rum.

Cointreau: Made from a neutral grain spirit, as opposed to Cognac. An aromatic flavour of natural citrus fruits. A great mixer or delightful over ice.

Creme de Cacao Dark: Rich, deep chocolate. Smooth and classy. Serve on its own, or mix for all kinds of delectable treats.

Creme de Cacao White: This liqueur delivers a powerfully lively, full bodied chocolate flavour. Excellent ingredient when absence of colour is desired.

Creme de Grand Marnier: A blend of Grand Marnier and smooth French cream. A premium product, a very smooth taste with the orange/cognac flavour blending beautifully with smooth cream. Introduced to Australia in 1985.

Creme de Menthe Green: Clear peppermint flavour, reminiscent of a fresh, crisp, clean winter's day in the mountains. Excellent mixer, a necessity in the gourmet kitchen.

Creme de Menthe White: As Creme de Menthe Green, when colour is not desired.

Curacao Blue: Same as Triple Sec, brilliant blue colour is added to make some cocktails more exciting.

Curacao Orange: Again, same as above, but stronger in orange, colouring is used for other varieties of cocktail mixers.

Curacao Triple Sec: Based on natural citrus fruits. Well known fact is citrus fruits are the most important aromatic flavour constituents. Interesting to know citrus fruit was known 2,000 years before Christ. As a liqueur one of the most versatile. Can be enjoyed with or without ice as a neat drink, or used in mixed cocktails more than any other liqueur. Triple Sec – also known as White Curacao.

Galliano: The distinguished taste! A classic liqueur that blends with a vast array of mixed drinks.

Gin: Its aroma comes from using the highest quality juniper berries and other rare and subtle herbs. Perfect mixer for both short and long drinks.

Kirsch: A fruit brandy distilled from morello cherries.
Delicious drunk straight and excellent in a variety of food recipes.

Drambuie: A Scotch whisky liqueur. Made from a secret recipe dating back to 1745. "Dram Buidheach" the drink that satisfies.

Frangelico: A precious liqueur imported from Italy. Made from wild hazelnuts with infusions of berries and flowers to enrich the flavour.

Grand Marnier: An original blend of fine old Cognac and an extract of oranges. The recipe is over 150 years old

Kahlúa: A smooth, dark liqueur made from real coffee and fine clear spirits. Its origins are based in Mexico.

Malibu: A clear liqueur based on white rum with the subtle addition of coconut. Its distinctive taste blends naturally with virtually every mixer available.

Melon Liqueur: Soft green, exudes freshness. Refreshing and mouth- watering honeydew melon. Simple yet complex. Smooth on the palate, serve on the rocks, or use to create summertime cocktails.

Ouzo: The traditional spirit aperitif of Greece. The distinctive flavour is derived mainly from the seed of the anise plant. A neutral grain spirit, flavoured with anise and distilled in Australia.

Peach: The flavour of fresh peaches and natural peach juice make this cocktail lover's dream.

Peachtree Schnapps: Crystal clear, light liqueur, bursting with the taste of ripe peaches. Drink chilled or on the rocks or mix with any soft drink or juice.

Pineapple: A just ripe, sun-filled delight. Delicious neat, a necessity for summertime cocktails.

Rum: A smooth, dry, light bodied rum, especially suited for drinks in which you require subtle aroma and delicate flavour.

Rye Whiskey: Distilled from corn, rye and malted barley. A light, mild and delicate Whiskey, ideal for drinking straight or in mixed cocktails.

Sabra: A unique flavour which comes from tangy jaffa oranges, with a hint of chocolate.

Sambuca – Clear: The Italian electric taste experience. Made from elderberries with a touch of anise.

Sambuca – Black: An exciting encounter between Sambuca di Galliano and extracts of black elderberry.

Scotch Whisky – A blended whisky.

Southern Comfort: A liqueur not a bourbon as often thought. It is unique, full-bodied liquor with a touch of sweetness. Its recipe is a secret, but it is known to be based on peaches and apricots. It is the largest selling liqueur in Australia.

Strawberry: Fluorescent red, unmistakable strawberry bouquet. Natural liqueur delivers a true to nature, fresh strawberry flavour.

Tennessee Whiskey : Contrary to popular belief, this is not a bourbon, it is a distinctive product called Tennessee Whiskey. Made from the 'old sour mash' process. Leached through hard maple charcoal, then aged in charred white oak barrels, at a controlled temperature, acquiring its body, bouquet and colour, yet remaining smooth.

Tequila: Distilled from the Mexcal variety of the cacti plant.
A perfect mixer or drink straight with salt and lemon.

Tia Maria: A liqueur with a cane spirit base, and its flavour derived from the finest Jamaican coffee. It is not too sweet with a subtle taste of coffee.

Vandermint: A rich chocolate liqueur with the added zest of mint.

Vermouth: By description, Vermouth is a herbally infused wine. Three styles are most prevalent, these are:

> **Rosso:** A bitter sweet herbal flavour, often drunk as an aperitif.

> **Bianco:** Is light, fruity and refreshing. Mixes well with soda, lemonade and fruit juices.

> **Dry:** Is crisp, light and dry and is used as a base for many cocktails.

Vodka: The second largest selling spirit in the world. Most Vodkas are steeped in tanks containing charcoal, removing all odours and impurities, making a superior quality product.

Triple Sec: See Blue Curacao.

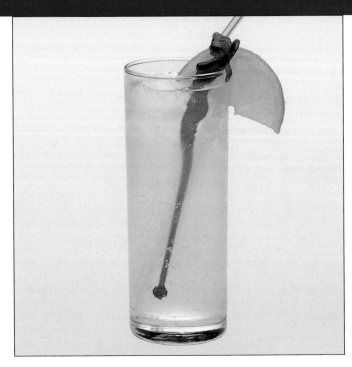

ASBSOLUT Cosmopolitan

Ingredients
Glass: 90mL/3 oz Martini Glass (chilled)
Mixers: 45mL/1½ oz ABSOLUT CITRON
              20mL/⅔ oz Triple Sec Liqueur
              20mL/⅔ oz Cranberry Classic
              juice of ½ fresh lime

Method
Shake with ice and strain into chilled martini glass.

Mixers: With orange twist.

Comments: A citrus tasting masterpiece. A very pleasant cocktail, destined to be a classic.

ASBSOLUT Iceberg

Ingredients
Glass: 285mL/10 oz Highball Glass
Mixers: 30mL/1 oz ABSOLUT CITRON
              15mL/½ oz Triple Sec Liqueur
              150mL/5 oz Bitter lemon

Method
Pour ABSOLUT CITRON and Triple Sec over ice into a chilled highball glass and top with Bitter Lemon.

Garnish: Orange slice

Comments: A delightful long citrus drink for a hot day.

Aqua Thunder

Ingredients

Glass: 285mL/10 oz Hi-Ball Glass

Mixers: 10mL/¹/₃ oz Blue Curacao Liqueur
10mL/¹/₃ oz Banana Liqueur
30mL/1 oz Melon Liqueur
10mL/¹/₃ oz freshly squeezed lemon
top-up with soda water

Method

Build over ice.

Garnish: Swizzle stick, and slice of lemon.

Comments: Watch in wonder as the soda waterfall splashes over the ice creating a thunderous aqua-coloured spectacular.

Australian Gold

Ingredients

Glass: 90mL/3 oz Cocktail Glass

Mixers: 30mL/1 oz Rum
30mL/1 oz Mango Liqueur
30mL/1 oz Galliano

Method

Build over ice.

Garnish: 1 small pineapple wedge.

Comments: This straight spirit cocktail is also known as "Queensland Wine".

B & B

Ingredients
Glass: Brandy Balloon
Mixers: 30mL/1 oz Martell Cognac
30mL/1 oz Benedictine

Method
Build, no ice.
Garnish: None.
Comments: Tempt your pallet with this historical blend of choice liqueurs. Relaxing by the fire on winter nights, the genuine connoisseur will enjoy interesting conversation with friends. Ideal with coffee.

Banana Colada

Ingredients
Glass: 300mL/10 oz Fancy Glass
Mixers: 30mL/1 oz Bacardi
30mL/1 oz Sugar syrup
30mL/1 oz Coconut cream
30mL/1 oz Cream
120m/4 oz Pineapple juice
$^1/_2$ Banana

Method
Build with ice and pour.
Garnish: Slice of banana, pineapple spear and mint leaves. Serves with straws.
Comments: A simple exemplary cocktail to demonstrate the variety of fruits available, particularly in Australia. Be adventurous and surprise yourself!

Banana Daiquiri

Ingredients
Glass: 140mL/5 oz Champagne Saucer
Mixers: ¾ Banana
30mL/1 oz Sugar syrup
30mL/1 oz Bacardi
30mL/1 oz Lemon juice

Method
Blend with ice and strain.
Garnish : Round slice of banana and mint leaves.
Comments : Frequently served on arrival at cocktail parties, this icy cold mixture is always warmly received by guests. Simple to prepare in large quantities, different combinations of fruits can be added to the base mix without deliberation. Adjust measurements of lemon and sugar accordingly for a sweeter or sour taste. Where unripe fruit is used, fruit liqueurs will enrich the flavour.

Bananarama

Ingredients
Glass: 140mL/5 oz Cocktail Glass
Mixers: 30mL/1 oz Vodka
30mL/1 oz Kahlúa
15mL/½ oz Baileys Irish Cream
1 Banana
60mL/2 oz Cream

Method
Blend with ice and pour.
Garnish: Two banana wheel slices wedged on rim of glass.
Comments: A delightful cocktail, drunk on the North Queensland island resorts, where tourists dance the "RAMA".

11

Between The Sheets

Ingredients
Glass: 140mL/5 oz Champagne Saucer
Mixers: 30mL/1 oz Brandy
30mL/1 oz Bacardi
30mL/1 oz Cointreau
15mL/1/2 oz Lemon juice

Method
Shake with ice and strain.
Garnish: Garnish with lemon slice and twist.
Comments: A pre-dinner cocktail. A fine blend of traditional spirits for the mature pallet. It may be served with a lemon twist.

Black Opal

Ingredients
Glass: 90mL/3 oz Cocktail Glass
Mixers: 15mL/1/2 oz Black Sambuca
15mL/1/2 oz Cointreau
15mL/1/2 oz Baileys Irish Cream
15mL/1/2 oz Cream

Method
Build Black Sambuca and Cointreau then light. Next, pour Baileys and Cream over flaming ingredients.
Garnish: None.
Comments: A novel demonstration of lifestyle cocktails - the heat of the flame illuminates the Black Opal.

Black Russian

Ingredients
Glass: 210mL/7 oz Old Fashioned Glass
Mixers: 30mL/1 oz Vodka
             30mL/1 oz Kahlúa

Method
Build over ice.
Garnish: Swizzle stick.
Comments: Superb after dinner as Vodka lubricates the way for the scrumptious chocolate Kahlúa.
A dollop of cream on top of the cola in a Hi-Ball glass to stretch the drink.
Tia Maria or Dark Creme de Caco may be substituted for Creme de Cafe, making the drink a **"Black Pearl".**

Bloody Mary

Ingredients
Glass: 285ml/10oz Hi-Ball Glass
Mixers: 30mL/1 oz Vodka
             Worchestershire sauce to taste
             125mL/4 oz Tomato juice
             Tabasco sauce to taste
             Salt and pepper to taste
             Celery salt, optional

Method
Build or shake over ice and strain
Garnish: Stick of celery, slice of lemon.
Comments: Remember to add the spice's first, then Vodka and followed by Tomato juice. Lemon juice and slices are optional ingredients. The celery stick is not part of the garnish, so feel free to nibble as you drink. The glass may also be salt-rimmed. A **"Virgin Mary"** is non alcoholic, with no vodka added. A "Bloody Maria" replaces Vodka with Tequila. Referred to as a **"Stomach Settler"** or **"Livener"**.

Blue Bayou

Ingredients

Glass: 285mL/10 oz Hi-Ball Glass
Mixers: 15mL/¹/₂ oz Galliano
15mL/¹/₂ oz Dry Vermouth
30mL/1 oz Gin
15m/¹/₂ oz Blue Curacao
top-up with lemonade (7-up)

Method

Shake with ice and pour.
Garnish: Lemon wheel and mint leaves.
Swizzle stick and straws.
Comments: A prize winning cocktail. Very refreshing cocktail. Perfect for outdoor parties. The yellow of the Galliano can tend to turn the Blue Curacao slightly aqua-green in colour.

Blueberry Delight

Ingredients

Glass: 140mL/5 oz Cocktail Glass
Mixers: 30mL/1 oz Black Sambuca
20mL/²/₃ oz Coconut Liqueur
10m/¹/₃ oz Strawberry Liqueur
60mL/2 oz Cream

Method

Shake with ice and strain.
Garnish: Strawberry on side of glass with blueberries on a toothpick.
Comments: Find your thrills on these Strawberry and Blueberry hills.

Blue French

Ingredients
Glass: 285mL/10 oz Hi-Ball Glass
Mixers: 30mL/1 oz Pernod
1 teaspoon Blue Curacao Liqueur
1 teaspoon Lemon juice
top-up with Bitter lemon

Method
Build over ice and stir.

Garnish: Lemon slice on side of glass, swizzle stick and straws.

Comments: A great thirst quencher. Ideal when relaxing by the pool. The publisher's favourite drink.

Blue Hawaii

Ingredients
Glass: 285mL/10 oz Hi-Ball Glass
Mixers: 30mL/1 oz Bacardi
30mL/1 oz Blue Curacao Liqueur
60mL/2 oz Pineapple juice
30mL/1 oz Lemon juice
30mL/1 oz Sugar syrup

Method
Build over ice and pour.

Garnish: Pineapple wedge, mint and cherry.
Serve with straws.

Comments: A favourite Hawaiian drink. The mixing of Pineapple juice and Blue Curacao tends to turn the cocktail aqua-green in colour.

Bosom Caresser

Ingredients
Glass: 140mL/5oz Champagne Saucer
Mixers: 30mL/1 oz Brandy
15mL/½ oz Orange Liqueur
1 teaspoon Grenadine Cordial
1 Egg yolk

Method
Shake with ice and strain.

Garnish: Two red cherries, slit on side of glass.

Comments: Close to every lady's heart! Egg yolk allows the cocktail to breathe supporting the Brandy's body and bounce. Fine on any occasion.

Brandy Alexander

Ingredients
Glass: 140mL/5 oz Champagne Saucer
Mixers: 30mL/1 oz Brandy
30mL/1 oz Dark Creme de Cacao Liqueur
1 teaspoon Grenadine Cordial
30mL/1 oz Cream

Method
Shake with ice and strain.

Garnish: Sprinkle of nutmeg and a cherry.

Comments: An after-dinner cocktail. See 'Helpful Hints' for an easy step-by-step guide on 'How To Make A Brandy Alexander Cross'.

An **"Alexander"** replaces the Cacao with Green Creme de Menthe.

Cognac may be substituted for Brandy to deliver an exceptional after taste.

Cafe Nero

Ingredients
Glass: 140mL/5 oz Champagne Saucer
Mixers: 30mL/1 oz Galliano
                Black Coffee
                fresh Cream
                Sugar

Method
Build, no ice.

Garnish: Grated chocolate.

Comments: Named after Emperor Nero of Rome. Firstly, sprinkle white sugar inside the glass after coating with Galliano. Set Galliano alight and twirl the glass so that flames burn brightly. Pour black coffee gently into glass then layer cream on top of the burning coffee. Sprinkle grated chocolate over the coffee. Also called a **"Roman Coffee"**. Coffee may be served on an accompanying saucer with marshmellows.

Cherries Jubilee

Ingredients
Glass: 140mL/5 oz Cocktail Glass
Mixers: 30mL/1 oz Cherry Advocaat
                30mL/1 oz White Creme deCacao
                15mL/$\frac{1}{2}$ oz Malibu
                40mL/1$\frac{1}{3}$ oz Cream
                15mL/$\frac{1}{2}$ oz Milk

Method
Shake with ice and strain.

Garnish: Grated chocolate and cherry and coconut rind on side of glass

Comments: Created by Leah Johns and won first place in Seagram's National Liqueur Championships, Hobart, Tasmania in 1990.

Chivas Manhattan

Ingredients

Glass: 90mL/3oz Cocktail Glass

Mixers: 1 shot Chivas Regal Scotch Whiskey
$^1/_2$ shot Dry Vermouth
$^1/_2$ shot Sweet Vermouth
dash of Grand Mariner
Burnt Orange Zest

Method

Place ice cubes in glass, pour in Chivas Regal, Dry & Sweet Vermouth and a dash of Grand Marnier. Stir thoroughly and strain into another chilled glass. Slice a piece of orange peel, set fire to the squeezed zest and place in the glass and enjoy.

Garnish: None

Comments: An interesting change to a "traditional" Manhattan cocktail.

Chivas Royal

Ingredients

Glass: Champagne Flute

Mixers: 1 shot Chivas Regal Scotch Whiskey
1 dash Apple Schnapps
Ginger Ale

Method

Half fill a chilled champagne flute with crushed ice. Pour in Chivas Regal, add Apple Schnapps (or clear apple juice if preferred). Top up with Ginger Ale.

Garnish: Place a slice of green apple into the drink and serve.

Comments: A drink fit for a King.

Daiquiri

Ingredients
Glass: 140mL/5 oz Champagne Saucer
Mixers: 45mL/1½ oz Rum
                30mL/ oz Pure Lemon Juice
                15mL/½ oz Sugar syrup
                ½ egg white, optional

Method
Shake with ice and strain.

Garnish: Lemon slice or lemon spiral.

Comments: Most Australian cocktail bars do not use egg white, however it definitely enhances the Daiquiri's appearance. Ideal for large parties as batches can be stored ready for instant use. Mango, when in season, is very popular. When mixing a pure fruit daiquiri, it is best to use an electric blender and blend well with ice, then strain into a champagne saucer.

Death In The Afternoon

Ingredients
Glass: 140mL/5oz Champagne Flute
Mixers: 15mL/½ oz Pernod
                Champagne

Method
Build, no Ice.

Garnish: None.

Comments: Ernest Hemingway's favourite cocktail. A bubbly occasion deserves this fully imported French aphrodisiac mixer.

Depth Charge

Ingredients
Glass: 425mL/14 oz Schooner Beer Glass
                 20mL/²/₃ oz Liqueur Glass
Mixers: 400mL/13 oz Beer
                 20mL/²/₃ oz Drambuie*

Method
Build, no ice
Garnish: None
Comments: Fill schooner, pot or beer mug with beer 3-5 centimetres below the glass rim. Toast by touching liqueur glasses filled with Drambuie before sliding into the beer glass. You'll be amazed that the Drambuie remains in the liqueur glass due to its higher density.
*Drambuie may be substituted with Lochan Ora.

Double Jeopardy

Ingredients
Glass: 285mL/10 oz Hi-Ball Glass
Mixers: 45mL/1¹/₂ oz Frangelico
                 45mL/1¹/₂ oz Black Sambuca
                 scoop of Vanilla ice cream
                 top-up with Milk

Method
Blend with Ice and Stir.
Garnish: Scooper spoon (long teaspoon) and straws.
Comments: Take a chance on this cocktail. Remember you can't be tried for the same crime twice. Great in winter by the open fire.

El Burro

Ingredients

Glass: 285mL/10 oz Fancy Cocktail Glass

Mixers: 15mL/½ oz Kahlúa
15mL/½ oz Rum
30mL/1 oz Coconut cream
30mL/1 oz Cream
½ Banana

Method

Blend with ice and strain.

Garnish: Banana and mint leaves.

Comments: A full and thick style of cocktail, very popular at the moment. Definitely and afternoon cocktail.

Evergreen

Ingredients

Glass: 90mL/3 oz Cocktail Glass

Mixers: 15mL/½ oz Dry Vermouth
30mL/1 oz Dry Gin
15mL/½ oz Melon Liqueur
1 teaspoon Blue Curacao Liqueur

Method

Stir over ice and strain.

Garnish: Red cherry on lip of glass

Comments: Stir the first three ingredients of this pre-dinner cocktail over ice and strain into cocktail glass. Then drop the Blue Curacao creating a visible layer. A poignant tasting cocktail consumed in summer.

Fallen Angel (Australian Version)

Ingredients

Glass: 285mL/10 oz Hi-Ball Glass
Mixers: 20mL/²/₃ oz Advocaat Liqueur
20mL/²/₃ oz Cherry Brandy
top-up with lemonade (7-up)

Method

Build over ice and stir.

Garnish: Red cherry or strawberry. Serve with straws.

Comments: Although requiring individual taste bud approval, ensure Advocaat and Cherry Brandy is mixed thoroughly before topping up with Lemonade (7-up). A **"Ruptured Rooster"** doesn't require the ingredients to be mixed.

Fluffy Duck (No. 1)

Ingredients

Glass: 285mL/10 oz Hi-Ball Glass
Mixers: 30mL/1 oz Rum
30mL/1 oz Advocaat Liqueur
top-up with lemonade (7-up)
cream, floated

Method

Build over ice.

Garnish: Orange slice and a red cherry. Serve with straws.

Comments: Most cocktail bars shake ingredients with cream before topping up with lemonade (7-up). When using a post mix gun, squirt the lemonade (7-up) directly into the middle of the liquid surface instead of spraying against the back of the glass. This gives a billowing cloud effect.

Fluffy Duck (No. 2)

Ingredients

Glass: 140mL/5 oz Champagne Saucer
Mixers: 30mL/1 oz Rum
               30mL/1 oz Advocaat
               30mL/1 oz Orange juice
               30mL/1 oz Cream

Method

Shake with ice and strain.

Garnish: Orange slice and a red cherry.

Comments: An after-dinner variation of the popular Fluffy Duck cocktail. A smoother and shorter drink.

Frappe

Ingredients

Glass: 90mL/3 oz Cocktail Glass
Mixers: 30mL/1 oz of preferred liqueur
               (e.g. Green Crème de Menthe Liqueur)

Method

Build over crushed ice.

Garnish: Two short straws

Comments: Spoon the required quantity of crushed ice into the glass. Create spectacular rainbow effects with small quantities of liqueurs. Green Crème de Menthe is highly recommended because it acts as a breath freshener after dessert.

Freddy-Fud-Pucker

Ingredients

Glass: 285mL/10 oz Hi-Ball Glass
Mixers: 30mL/1 oz Tequila
               120mL/4 oz Orange juice
               15mL/½ oz Galliano, floated

Method

Build over ice.

Garnish: Orange slice and red cherry.
Serve with straws.

Comments: Fantastic when drinking with friends – each participant after drinking half the cocktail says very quickly, 3 times. "Freddy Fud Puckers Fud any Puck". The first to be caught out is obliged to buy the next round. Be sure to mind your 'p's and 'f's when ordering.

French Fantasy

Ingredients

Glass: 140mL/5 oz Cocktail Glass
Mixers: 30mL/1 oz Creme de Grand Marnier
               30mL/1 oz Vodka
               15mL/½ oz Tia Maria
               30mL/1 oz Pineapple juice
               30mL/1 oz Orange juice

Method

Shake with ice and strain.

Garnish: Banana slice and red cherry.

Comments: Creme de Grand Marnier is similar to Bailey's. This cocktail is really smooth and easy to drink.

God Daughter

Ingredients
Glass: 140mL/5 oz Champagne Saucer
Mixers: 30mL/1 oz Sambuca
             30mL/1 oz Amaretto di Saronno
             30mL/1 oz Cream
             1 teaspoon Grenadine Cordial

Method
Shake with ice and strain.
Garnish: Chocolate flake, strawberry and mint.
Comments: Ideal cocktail after Italian food.

God Father

Ingredients
Glass: 185mL/6 oz Old Fashioned Spirit Glass
Mixers: 30mL/1 oz Scotch Whisky
             30mL/1 oz Amaretto di Saronno

Method
Build over ice.
Garnish: None
Comments: To be drunk as either a pre-dinner drink or a night-cap. The guiding hand of Amaretto tempers the boldness of the Scotch.

Golden Cadillac

Ingredients
Glass: 140mL/5 oz Cocktail Glass
Mixers: 30mL/1 oz Galliano
30mL/1 oz White Crème de Cacao
Liqueur
30mL/1 oz Cream

Method
Shake with ice and strain.

Garnish: Red cherry or strawberry

Comments: The distilled Cocoa Beans will take you for the ride of your life. Cruise through this cocktail in luxurious style. Essential for all cocktail parties. Anywhere, anytime.

Golden Dream

Ingredients
Glass: 140mL/5 oz Cocktail Glass
Mixers: 30mL/²/₃ oz Galliano
20mL/²/₃ oz Cointreau*
20mL/²/₃ oz Orange Juice
20mL/²/₃ oz Cream

Method
Shake with ice and strain.

Garnish: Red cherry on a toothpick on side of glass.

Comments: Chilled Orange juice tarts the Galliano and freezes the Cointreau leaving a creamy tangy lining from your throat to your toes. Cointreau may be replaced with Triple Sec.

Gomango

Ingredients

Glass: 440mL/14 oz Hurricane Glass
Mixers: 15mL/½ oz Triple Sec Liqueur
15mL/½ oz White Crème de Cacao
15mL/½ oz Cherry Advocaat Liqueur
15mL/½ oz Orange juice
15mL/½ oz Cream
1 cheek of fresh Mango

Method

Blend with ice.
Garnish: Butterfly strawberry on side of glass.
Comments: Created by Con Pandelakia, winner of 1991 Australian Title.

Grasshopper

Ingredients

Glass: 140mL/5 oz champagne Saucer
Mixers: 30mL/1 oz Crème de Menthe Liqueur
30mL/1 oz White Crème de Cacao
30mL/1 oz Cream

Method

Shake with ice and strain.
Garnish: 2 red cherries slit on the side of the glass.
Comments: Jump right into this very popular after dinner cocktails. Some people prefer Dark Crème de Cacao instead of White Crème de Cacao. Shake until smooth

G.R.B.

Ingredients

Glass: 90mL/3 oz Cocktail Glass

Mixers: 30mL/1 oz Galliano

10mL/^{1}/$_3$ oz Grenadine Cordial

30mL/1 oz Rum

Method

Build over ice.

Garnish: Float 1 mint leaf.

Comments: Anyone who stalls gets a double-hit-round. The mint permeates the Rum leaving a refreshingly sweet aftertaste. Please use your imagination to name this acronym!

Green with Envy

Ingredients

Glass: 210mL/7 oz Hurricane Glass

Mixers: 30mL/1 oz Ouzo

30mL/1 oz Blue Curacao Liqueur

120mL/4 oz Pineapple juice

Method

Shake with ice and pour.

Garnish: Pineapple spear with leaves and cherry. Serve with straws.

Comments: An afternoon cocktail. The aniseed in Ouzo chills the pungent Pineapple Juice. As they say... Jealousy's a curse, Envy is worse.

Irish Coffee

Ingredients
Glass: 250mL/8 oz Irish Coffee Glass
Mixers: 30mL/1 oz Baileys Irish Cream
               1 teaspoon brown sugar
               top-up with hot black coffee
               float fresh Cream

Method
Build (no ice).
Garnish: Chocolate flake optional.
Comments: The most widely drunk liqueur coffee which verifies its approval amongst coffee lovers. Tullamore Dew & Jameson's are most popular Irish Whiskies. Other liqueur coffees are: **French – Brandy, English – Gin, Russian – Vodka, American – Bourbon, Calypso – Dark Rum, Jamaican – Tia Maria, Parisienne – Grand Marnier, Mexican – Kahlúa, Monks – Benedictine, Scottish –**

Harvey Wallbanger

Ingredients
Glass: 285mL/9 oz Hi-Ball Glass
Mixers: 40mL/1 1/3 oz Vodka
               125mL/4 oz Orange Juice
               15mL/1/2 oz Galliano, floated

Method
Build over ice.
Garnish: Orange slice and cherry.
Swizzle stick and straws.
Comments: The local Hawaiian bartenders will tell you a visiting Irishman called Harvey pin-balled down the corridor to hotel room after a night out. Hence, he was known a "Harvey Wallbanger".

29

Scotch, Canadian – Rye.

Japanese Slipper

Ingredients

Glass: 90mL/3 oz Cocktail Glass

Mixers: 30mL/1 oz Melon Liqueur

              30mL/1 oz Cointreau

              30mL/1 oz Lemon juice

Method

Shake with ice and strain

Garnish: Slice of lemon on side of glass.

Comments: Simple to prepare and the habit preferences of consumers has ensured this cocktail will remain one most often requested. Pouring 1 teaspoon Grenadine upon completion of the cocktail gives a marvellous visual effect and sweetens the sour element.

Jelly Bean

Ingredients

Glass: 285mL/9 oz Hi-ball glass

Mixers: 30mL/1 oz Ouzo

              15mL/$\frac{1}{2}$ oz Blue Curacao Liqueur

              15mL/$\frac{1}{2}$ oz Grenadine Cordial

              Top-up with Lemonade (7-up)

Method

Build over ice.

Garnish: Swizzle stick and straws. Red cherry dropped into glass.

Comments: A cool liquid confectionery. Dropping Blue Curacao and Grenadine into the cocktail after presenting to the customer gives a swirling lollipop effect. Regularly drunk without the Blue Curacao.

Kamikaze

Ingredients
Glass: 140mL/5 oz Cocktail Glass
Mixers: 30mL/1 oz Vodka
30mL/1 oz Cointreau
30mL/1 oz fresh lemon juice
1 teaspoon Lime cordial

Method
Shake with ice and strain.
Garnish: Red cocktail onion on a toothpick in the glass.
Comments: Maintain freshness for larger volumes by adding stained egg white. Mix in a jug and keep refrigerated. For the hyper-active. Cointreau may be replaced with Triple Sec.

K.G.B.

Ingredients
Glass: 185mL/6 oz Old Fashioned Spirit Glass
Mixers: 30mL/1 oz Kahlúa
30mL/1 oz Grand Marnier
30mL/1 oz Baileys Irish Cream

Method
Build over ice.
Garnish: None
Comments: The first letter of each of the ingredients give this cocktail its name. A late night party drink.

Kick in the Balls

Ingredients
Glass: 140mL/5 oz Champagne Saucer
Mixers: 30mL/1 oz Rum
            30mL/1 oz Orange Juice
            30mL/1 oz Melon Liqueur
            30mL/1 oz Cream
            15mL/¹/₂ oz Coconut Cream

Method
Shake with ice and strain.
Garnish: Two melon balls previously marinated in the Coruba Rum.

Comments: Float melon balls. Using a toothpick, eat both balls together and you'll be sure to feel a "Kick in the Balls". Refrigerate melon balls to preserve their freshness.

Kir

Ingredients
Glass: 140mL/5 oz Wine Goblet
Mixers: 15mL/¹/₂ oz Cassis Liqueur
            Top-up with dry White Wine

Method
Build, no ice.
Garnish: None.
Comments: A superb pre-dinner drink. Use cold dry wines. Do not spoil the drink by using more than 15mL/¹/₂ oz of Cassis Liqueur. To make a "Kir Imperial" substitute 1 teaspoon Grenadine for 15mL/¹/₂ oz Cassis. "Kir Royale" is served in a 140mL/5 oz champagne flute with only 1 teaspoon Cassis liqueur and topped with the best champagne available. Always remember, the better the champagne, the better the drink.
Hint: Sprinkle a thumb pinch of sugar to produce fizzy

bubbles from the champagne. Served chilled.

Lady M

Ingredients

Glass: 285mL/9 oz Hurricane Glass

Mixers: 45mL/1½ oz Frangelico
45m/1½ oz Melon Liqueur
2 scoops vanilla ice cream

Garnish: Strawberry on side of glass sprinkled with grated chocolate.

Comments: Blend for more than 20 seconds to thoroughly mix ingredients. Be adventurous and try various flavoured ice-creams.

Lamborghini

Ingredients

Glass: 90mL/3 oz Cocktail Glass

Mixers: 20mL/⅔ oz Crème de Café Liqueur
20mL/⅔ oz Cointreau
20mL/⅔ oz Sambuca
Cold Fresh Cream

Method

Build, no ice.

Garnish: Grated chocolate flakes.

Comments: Layer ingredients in the above order using a spoon, then float fresh cream. As the name suggests, speed is the object of this cocktail. You may like to try drinking each layered ingredient through a straw at a quickening speed; similar to changing the gears in a Lamborgini.

Lamborghini (Flaming)

Ingredients
Glass: 4-6 Tall Dutch Cordial Glasses
Mixers: 20mL/²/₃ oz Kahlua
20mL/²/₃ oz Cointreau } per cocktail
20mL/²/₃ oz Sambuca
Cold Fresh cream

Method
Heat and build.

Garnish: Grated chocolate flake.

Comments: Warm alcoholic ingredients in a stainless steel saucepan. Be sure to simmer flame to avoid scorching Kahlua. Stand glasses in a row and allow flame to burn for 10-15 seconds. Pour cold cream into a spoon and float onto the cocktail to extinguish flame. The nightclub version replaces Sambuca for Green Chartreuse as it is distinct in colour, easier to layer and also flamed.

Long Island Iced Tea

Ingredients
Glass: 285mL/9 oz Hi-Ball Glass
Mixers: 30mL/1 oz Vodka
30mL/1 oz Lemon juice
30mL/1 oz Tequila
30mL/1 oz Sugar syrup
30mL/1 oz White Rum
dash of Cola
30mL/1 oz Cointreau

Method
Build over Ice.

Garnish: Lemon twist and mint leaves. Serve with straws.

Comments: The tea coloured cola is splashed into the cocktail making it slightly unsuitable for a "Tea Party". Many variations are concocted using different white spirits. American by design, Australians know it better as a **"Long Island Iced Tea"**. It is strongly recommended that you consume no more than one.

Madame Butterfly

Ingredients

Glass: 140mL/ 5oz Margarita Glass

Mixers:
1. 30mL/1 oz Passoa
   15mL/¹/₂ oz Melon Liqueur
   15mL/¹/₂ oz White Creme de Cacao
   30mL/1 oz Pineapple Juice
2. 30mL/1 oz Cream
   15mL/¹/₂ oz Melon Liqueur

Method

1. Shake with ice and strain.
2. Layered Melon Liqueur and Cream.

Garnish: Strawberry and Butterfly.

Comments: This cocktail requires two shakers. In one hand, shake the first four ingredients over ice and strain. In the other hand, shake Melon Liqueur and Cream, then layer. An innovative award winning cocktail.

Mai-Tai

Ingredients

Glass: 285mL/9 oz Hi-Ball Glass

Mixers:
30mL/1 oz Rum
30mL/1 oz Lemon juice
15mL/¹/₂ oz Amaretto di Saronno
30mL/1 oz Sugar syrup
15mL/¹/₂ oz Rum
¹/₂ fresh Lime juiced
30mL/1 oz Orange Curacao Liqueur

Method

Shake with ice and pour.

Garnish: Pineapple spear, mint leaves, tropical flowers if possible (e.g. Singapore Orchid), lime shell. Serve with straws.

Comments: A well known rum-based refreshing tropical cocktail. Grenadine is often added to redden a glowing effect while the Rum may be floated on top when served without straws. Rum lovers drink their Mai Tais this way. It can also be built into a tall glass and stirred with the pineapple spear.

35

Malibu Magic

Ingredients

Glass: 285mL/9 oz Hurricane Glass

Mixers: 30mL/1 oz Malibu*
30mL/1 oz Strawberry Liqueur
30mL/1 oz Orange juice
3-4 fresh strawberries
60mL/2 oz Cream

Method

Blend with ice and pour.

Garnish: A single strawberry and twisted orange peel.

Comments: Shake to the wonders of Californian dreaming. *Malibu may be substituted with Coconut Liqueur. 15ml of Cointreau may be added for that magic moment.

Margarita

Ingredients

Glass: 140mL/5 oz Margarita Glass, salt-rimmed

Mixers: 30mL/1 oz Tequila
30mL/1 oz Lemon Juice
15mL/$\frac{1}{2}$ oz Cointreau
$\frac{1}{2}$ egg white, optional

Method

Shake with Ice and Strain.

Garnish: Lemon wheel on edge of glass.

Comments: Margarita's can be 'shaken' or 'frozen' – a professional bartender will always ask which method is preferred. A "Frozen Margarita" (Sorbet) contains $\frac{1}{3}$ of the blender full of ice. Add water if the mix becomes gluggy.

Martini

Ingredients
Glass: 90mL/3 oz Cocktail Glass
Mixers: 45mL/1½ oz Gin
               20mL/⅔ oz Dry Vermouth

Method
Stir over ice and strain.
Garnish: Lemon twist or olive on toothpick in the glass.
Comments: The classically sophisticated black-tie cocktail. Always stirred, however, when shaken it is known as a **"Bradford"**. An olive garnish retains the Gin sting whereas a lemon twist makes the cocktail smoother.
Note: A "Dry Martini" has less Vermouth.

Midori Avalanche

Ingredients
Glass: 285mL/9 oz Hurricane Glass
Mixers: 30mL/1 oz Blue Curacao
               30mL/1 oz Melon Liqueur
               15mL/½ oz Triple Sec Liqueur
               60mL/2 oz Pineapple Juice

Method
Pour Blue Curacao into glass. Blend other ingredients with ice and pour.
Garnish: Triangle of pineapple on side of glass.
Comments: This deep sea cocktail can be found at pool bars around Australia. Be sure to use plenty of ice to quench a hot dry thirst.

Moscow Mule

Ingredients
Glass: 285mL/9 oz Hi-Ball Glass
Mixers: 30mL/1 oz Vodka
               15mL/1/2 oz lime cordial
               top-up with ginger beer

Method
Build over ice.

Garnish: Slice of lemon and mint. Straws and swizzle stick.

Comments: A long, cool, refreshing cocktail. It tastes a lot better if the juice of half a lime is squeezed into the cocktail in place of the lime cordial.

Mount Temple

Ingredients
Glass: 90mL/3 oz Cocktail Glass
Mixers: 30mL/1 oz Kahlúa
               30mL/1 oz Tequila
               30mL/1 oz Coconut Liqueur

Method
Build over ice.

Garnish: Dollop of cream in centre of glass.

Comments: Love is a temple and you'll love this higher ground.

Old Fashioned - Scotch

Ingredients

Glass: 285mL/9 oz Old Fashioned Spirit Glass

Mixers: 30mL/1 oz Scotch Whisky
Angostura Bitters
sugar cube
soda water

Method

Build over ice.

Garnish: ½ slice of orange and lemon and a cherry.
A swizzle stick may be used.

Comments: Splash Bitters evenly over the sugar cube before adding ice, Scotch and topping up with soda. A soothing 'knocking-off' drink after 5 pm. Ensure cherries are dry. If cherries are moist, the juice may taint the flavour, thereby marring the appearance of the Scotch. Bourbon and Rye Whisky may be served in the **"Old Fashioned"** way.

Ole

Ingredients

Glass: 90mL/3 oz Cocktail Glass

Mixers: 30mL/1 oz Tequila
30mL/1 oz Banana Liqueur
10mL/¹/₃ oz Blue Curacao Liqueur

Method

Stir over ice and strain.

Garnish: Lemon wheel

Comments: 1988 World Cocktail Championship winner. Stir the Tequila and Banana Liqueur gently over ice to avoid 'bruising' and strain into the glass, then drop Blue Curacao. It not only looks good but is great to drink. Easy to make if you're in a hurry.

Orgasm

Ingredients

Glass: 210mL/7 oz Old Fashioned Spirit Glass

Mixers: 20mL/²/₃ oz Baileys Irish Cream
20mL/²/₃ oz Cointreau

Method

Build over ice.

Garnish: Strawberry or cherries, optional

Comments: Probably the most widely drunk cocktail in Australia and very popular with the ladies.

A **"Multiple Orgasm"** is made with the addition of 30ml of fresh Cream or Milk.

A **"Screaming Multiple Orgasm"** has the addition of 15ml Galliano along with 30ml fresh Cream or Milk.

Palm Sundae

Ingredients

Glass: 285mL/9 oz Hurricane Glass

Mixers: 45mL/1¹/₂ oz Peach Liqueur
30mL/1 oz Coconut Liqueur
15mL/¹/₂ oz Banana Liqueur
60mL/2 oz Tropical Fruit Juice
3 fresh strawberries

Method

Blend with ice and pour.

Garnish: Orange wedge, pineapple leaves and Maraschino cherry.

Comments: Peach liqueur is dynamically exquisite in this specially designed cocktail recipe. The succulent peach flavour is another member in the new generation of natural tropical fruit cocktails.

Pimm's No. 1 Cup

Ingredients

Glass: 285mL/9oz Hi-Ball Glass

Mixers: 30-45ml Pimm's No. 1 Cup
top-up with either lemonade (7-up) or dry ginger or equal parts of both

Method

Build over ice.

Garnish: Orange and lemon slice, cherries, cucumber skin, swizzle stick and straws.

Comments: A slice of orange can detract from the sweet aftertaste. Slicing the inside of the cucumber skin allows the small drops to keep the drink chilled. Originally 6 Pimm's numbers were commonly consumed, today there are only two. Pimm's No.1 – Gin base, Pimm's No. 2 – Vodka base. Often referred to as the **"Fruit Cocktail Cocktail"**.

Pina Colada

Ingredients

Glass: 285mL/9 oz Hi-ball Glass

Mixers: 30mL/1 oz Rum
30mL/1 oz Coconut Cream
30mL/1 oz Sugar Syrup
125mL/4 oz Unsweetened Pineapple juice

Method

Shake with ice and pour.

Garnish: Pineapple wedge - three leaves and a cherry. Straws & swizzle stick.

Comments: Another tropical Hawaiian cocktail which is distinguished by including Coconut Cream. Unfortunately, it is not normally stocked by Australian bars. If temporarily unavailable, Coconut Liqueur will suffice. Cream is optional for a richer blend.

Pink Panther

Ingredients
Glass: 140mL/5 oz Champagne Saucer

Mixers: 22mL/⅔ oz Bourbon
30mL/1 oz Vodka
15mL/½ oz Malibu
40mL/1⅓ oz Cream
dash Grenadine

Method
Shake with ice and strain

Garnish: Cherry and mint.

Comments: Leap out of a 'pink fit' with one of the first coconut cocktails made in Australia. For the intrepid.

Prairie Oyster

Ingredients
Glass: 90mL/3 oz Cocktail Glass

Mixers: 30mL/1 oz Brandy
Salt and pepper
Worcestershire Sauce
Tabasco Sauce
1 Egg yolk

Method
Build, no ice.

Garnish: None

Comments: the spices relieve a sore head and the Brandy replenishes lost energy. Brandy may be replaced with any spirit of your choice, however cold Vodka is medically soothing. Best before breakfast.

Pretty Woman

Ingredients

Glass: 285mL/9 oz Hurricane Glass

Mixers: **Blender 1**
30mL/1 oz Melon Liqueur
30mL/1 oz Malibu
Blender 2
30mL/1 oz Strawberry Liqueur
3-4 strawberries

Method

Blend with ice in two separate blenders and pour.
Garnish: Strawberry and umbrella on side of glass.
Comments: Remember to tilt the glass when pouring the two sets of ingredients into the glass. Choosing a long glass will assist you. Very alcoholic as there is no juice. A kaleidoscope of colour for you to enjoy.

Raffles Singapore Sling

Ingredients

Glass: 285mL/9 oz Hi-Ball Glass

Mixers: 30mL/1 oz Gin
30mL/1 oz Orange juice
30mL/1 oz Cherry Brandy Liqueur
30mL/1 oz Lime juice
15mL/$^{1}/_{2}$ oz Triple Sec Liqueur
30mL/1 oz Pineapple juice
dash Angostura Bitters
15mL/$^{1}/_{2}$ oz Benedictine

Method

Shake with ice and pour.
Garnish: Orange slice, mint, a cherry, swizzle stick and straws.
Comments: This recipe is the original Singapore version, with its fruit juices it tastes totally different from some Gin Slings commonly served in bars.

Rocket Fuel

Ingredients
Glass: 210mL/7 oz Old Fashioned Spirit Glass
Mixers: 15mL/½ oz Rum
             15mL/½ oz Dry Gin
             15mL/½ oz Vodka
             30mL/1 oz Lemonade (7-up)
             15mL/½ oz Tequila

Method
Build over ice.
Garnish: Swizzle stick.
Comments: This cocktail secured it's bar fame when Australia's rock legend Jimmy Barnes sang about "sitting on the beach drinking Rocket Fuel...oh yeah!"

Rusty Nail

Ingredients
Glass: 210mL/7 oz Old Fashioned Spirit Glass
Mixers: 30mL/1 oz Scotch Whisky
             30mL/1 oz Drambuie

Method
Build over ice.
Garnish: Lemon twist (optional).
Comments: A traditional pillow softener for refined gentlemen. The highlands of Scotland's Drambuie ascends your spirit above the centre of the world. Lemon will diffuse the bite of the Scotch. Watch your step when ordering!

Salty Dog

Ingredients

Glass: 285mL/9 oz Hi-Ball Glass – Salt-rimmed

Mixers: 45mL/1½ oz Vodka
top-up with Grapefruit Juice

Method

Build over ice.

Garnish: Swizzle stick, straws optional.

Garnish: Slowly re-emerging as the long cool cocktail it was renowned for in its heyday. Unfortunately, a limited number of bars stock Grapefruit Juice, which restricts availability. But as the saying goes " Every dog has his day". Straws are unnecessary, drink the cocktail from the salt rim.

Satin Pillow

Ingredients

Glass: 140mL/5 oz Cocktail Glass

Mixers: 1 teaspoon Strawberry Liqueur
10mL/⅓ oz Cointreau
15mL/½ oz Frangelico
15mL/½ oz Tia Maria
20mL/⅔ oz Pineapple juice
20mL/⅔ oz Cream

Method

Blend with ice and pour.

Garnish: Cut a strawberry in half and place on side of glass then swirl cream over strawberry halves.

Comments: The very piquant taste is as smooth as satin bed linen.

Screwdriver

Ingredients

Glass: 210mL/7 oz Old Fashioned Spirit Glass
Mixers: 45mL/1½ oz Vodka
                45mL/1½ oz Orange juice

Method

Build over ice.

Garnish: Orange twist or spiral.

Comments: A frequently requested basic spirit mixed drink. Subtle at any time of day. The original recipe contains equal measurements of Vodka and Orange Juice.

A Comfortable Screw is made with 30mL/1 oz Vodka, 15mL/½ oz Southern Comfort topped with Orange Juice.

A Slow Comfortable Screw has added 15mL/½ oz Sloe Gin.

A Long Slow Comfortable Screw is a longer drink served in a 285mL/10 oz Hi-Ball glass.

A Long Slow Comfortable Screw Up Against A Wall has the addition of 15mL/½ oz Galliano floated.

Sex on the Beach

Ingredients

Glass: 210mL/7 oz Fancy Cocktail Glass
Mixers: 15mL/½ oz Kahlúa
                30mL/1 oz Malibu
                30mL/1 oz Pineapple Liqueur
                60mL/2 oz Cream

Method

Shake with ice and strain.

Garnish: Pineapple wedge on side of glass.

Comments: A most enjoyable cocktail when you fell mischievous.

Sidecar

Ingredients

Glass: 90mL/3 oz Cocktail Glass
Mixers: 30mL/1 oz Brandy
20mL/²/₃ oz Cointreau*
25mL/²/₃ oz Lemon Juice

Method

Shake with ice and strain.

Garnish: Lemon twist optional.

Comments: A zappy pre-dinner cocktail. The Lemon juice purifies the brandy and ferments the Cointreau. Too much Lemon Juice will leave an acidic after taste.

*Cointreau may be substituted with Triple Sec.

Snowball

Ingredients

Glass: 285mL/9 oz Hi-ball Glass
Mixers: 30mL/1 oz Advocaat Liqueur
Top-up with Lemonade (7-up)
Dash of Lime Cordial
Cream, optional

Method

Build over ice.

Garnish: Red cherry. Swizzle sticks and straws.

Comments: Place ice in the glass after mixing the Advocaat with Lemonade (7-up) before floating cream on top. The pressure of a post mix gun will create the desired 'snowball' effect.

Southern Peach

Ingredients

Glass: 140mL/5 oz Martini Glass
Mixers: 30mL/1 oz Cointreau
15mL/½ oz Brandy
15mL/½ oz Cherry Brandy Liqueur
15mL/½ oz Pineapple juice
15mL/½ oz Lemon juice

Method

Shake with ice and strain.

Garnish: Butterfly a strawberry, place on side of glass, twirl cream over strawberry and sprinkle over flaked chocolate.

Comments: A magical cocktail that can be 'fluffed' up by adding egg white.

South Pacific

Ingredients

Glass: 285mL/9 oz Hi-ball Glass
Mixers: 30mL/1 oz Dry Gin
15mL/½ oz Galliano
top with Lemonade (7-up)
15mL/½ oz Blue Curacao Liqueur

Method

Build over ice, then add the Blue Curacao last.

Garnish: Lemon slice and cherry, swizzle stick and straws.

Comments: Australia's first gold medal winning cocktail. Created by Gary Revell, to win the World Cocktail Championships in Yugoslavia in 1979.

Spritzer

Ingredients
Glass: 185mL/6oz Wine Goblet
Mixers: Dry White Wine, chilled
Soda Water

Method
Build, no ice.
Garnish: None.
Comments: "Wet the whistle" with a responsible alcoholic alternative. Ladies prefer the soda dilution although you may be asked for lemonade (7-up).

Splice

Ingredients
Glass: 210mL/7 oz Hurricane Glass
Mixers: 30mL/1 oz Melon Liqueur
15mL/1/2 oz Galliano
15mL/1/2 oz Coconut Liqueur
30mL/1 oz Pineapple juice
30mL/1 oz Cream

Method
Blend with ice and pour.
Garnish: Pineapple wedge and leaves on side of glass.
Comments: Enjoyed in Australia for several years. The smooth, well blended flavour has ensured this cocktails ever increasing admiration.

Stars & Stripes

Ingredients

Glass: 300mL/10 oz Fancy Cocktail Glass

Mixers: 10mL/⅓ oz Blue Curacao

Blender 1
30mL/1 oz Southern Comfort
30mL/1 oz Frangelico

Blender 2
30mL/1 oz Strawberry Liqueur
3-4 Strawberries

Method

Pour Blue Curacao into glass. Blend other ingredients with ice in 2 separate blenders and pour.

Garnish: Sprinkle grated chocolate flakes over top and add a strawberry and USA flag to side of glass.

Comments: Remember to tilt the glass when pouring the two sets of ingredients.

Stinger

Ingredients

Glass: 90mL/3 oz Cocktail Glass

Mixers: 45mL/1½ oz Brandy
10mL/⅓ oz White Crème de Menthe

Method

Stir over ice and strain.

Garnish: None.

Comments: The distinct minty aroma of White Crème de Menthe prevades this prefect pre-dinner cocktail. The Brandy delivers the sting!

Strawberry Blonde

Ingredients

Glass: 285mL/9 oz Hi-Ball Glass

Mixers: 30mL/1 oz Dark Creme de Cacao
top-up with cola
fresh cream, floated
splash of Grenadine

Method

Build over ice.

Garnish: A red cherry. Swizzle sticks and straws.

Comments: Tasting this cocktail will reveal the secret why 'blondes have more fun'. Placing ice in the glass after mixing the Carao with Cola will support the floating cream on top. A dessert cocktail. Ideal on a blind date.

Summer Breeze

Ingredients

Glass: 300mL/10 oz Fancy Cocktail Glass

Mixers: 60ml/2oz Peach Tree Liqueur
15mL/$\frac{1}{2}$ oz Rum
15mL/$\frac{1}{2}$ oz Mango Liqueur
15mL/$\frac{1}{2}$ oz Gin
60mL/2 oz Pineapple juice
60mL/2 oz Orange juice
1 fresh Mango
1 fresh Peach

Method

Blend with ice and pour.

Garnish: Half an orange slice and orange peel twist.

Comments: With temperature hot and humidity high, this is often the only breeze available in the afternoon.

Sunken Treasure

Ingredients

Glass: 90mL/3 oz Cocktail Glass

Mixers: 30mL/1 oz Gin
15mL/½ oz Peach Liqueur
Champagne to top-up
apricot conserve

Method

Stir over ice, strain and top-up.

Garnish: Place a teaspoon of apricot conserve in the bottom of glass and then push a strawberry into conserve.

Comments: It is always pleasing to include innovative cocktail garnishes. Stir Gin and Peach Liqueur over ice and strain, then top glass with champagne. 1989 Australian National Cocktail winner.

Sweet Lady Jane

Ingredients

Glass: 140mL/5 oz Champagne Saucer

Mixers: 15mL/½ oz Grand Marnier
15mL/½ oz Orange Juice
15mL/½ oz Cointreau
15mL/½ oz Coconut Cream
30mL/1 oz Strawberry Liqueur
30mL/1 oz fresh cream

Method

Shake with ice and strain.

Garnish: Strawberry, mint and chocolate flakes.

Comments: An orange glazed cocktail gorgeously presented with chocolate flakes that swirl the coconut and strawberry liqueurs.

Sweet Martini

Ingredients
Glass: 90mL/3 oz Cocktail Glass
Mixers: 45mL/1½ oz Dry Gin
                20ml/⅔ oz Rosso Vermouth

Method
Stir over ice and strain.
Garnish: Red cherry on toothpick in glass.
Comments: Sister to the "Dry Martini", the sweeter Vermouth overwhelms the Gin sting. A pre-dinner cocktail which can be stirred and strained either:
"On The Rocks" - served in a standard Spirit glass over ice.
"Straight Up" - served in a 90ml Cocktail Glass over ice.

Tequila Slammer

Ingredients
Glass: 185mL/6 oz Old Fashioned Spirit glass
Mixers: 30mL/1 oz Tequila
                60mL/2 oz Dry Ginger Ale

Method
Build, no ice.
Garnish: None.
Comments: A one hit wonder - holding a coaster over the entire rim, rotate the glass clockwise on the bar 4-5 times. Lift and 'slam' the base of the glass down onto the bar, then skol in one shot. The carbonated mixer fizzes the Tequila when slammed.
Usually bartenders splash only 5-10ml of Dry Ginger Ale to aid the quick drinking process.

Tequila Sunrise

Ingredients
Glass: 285mL/9 oz Hi-Ball Glass
Mixers: 30mL/1 oz Tequila
1 teaspoon Grenadine
top-up with Orange juice

Method
Build over ice.
Garnish: Orange wheel, a red cherry.
Swizzle stick and straws.
Comments: Sipping this long cool cocktail at sunrise or sunset is magnificent.
To obtain the cleanest visual effect, drop Grenadine down the inside of the glass, after topping up with Orange Juice. Dropping Grenadine in the middle creates a fallout effect, detracting from the presentation of the cocktail.
Best served with chilled, freshly squeezed oranges.

The Dik Hewett

Ingredients
Glass: 140mL/5 oz Cocktail Glass
Mixers: 30mL/1 oz Jack Daniel's Old No. 7
30mL/1 oz Cognac
30mL/1 oz Benedictine
glass of water (on the side)

Method
Shake with ice and strain.
Garnish: None
Comments: The late arrival cocktail. Sure to test, sure to please.

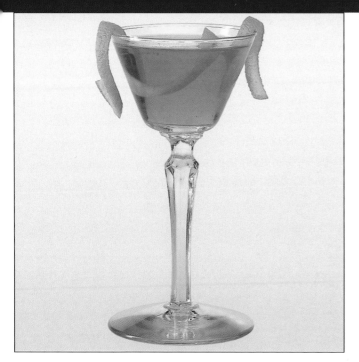

T.N.T.

Ingredients

Glass: 90mL/3 oz Cocktail Glass
Mixers: 45mL/1½ oz Brandy
              20mL/⅔ oz Orange Liqueur
              dash of Pernod
              dash of Angostura Bitters

Method

Stir over ice and strain.

Garnish: Orange twist.

Comments: A powder keg, really a cocktail to liven up the party. Drink in moderation, as this one can really cause a "bang".

Toblerone

Ingredients

Glass: 140ml/5 oz Cocktail Glass
Mixers: 1 teaspoon Baileys Irish Cream
              15mL/½ oz Kahlúa
              15mL/½ oz White Creme de Cacao
              30mL/1 oz Frangelico
              60mL/2 oz Cream
              ½ teaspoon Honey

Method

Blend with ice and pour.

Garnish: Sprinkle almond flakes and nutmeg over top. To create a special effect drag a cotton strand over completed cocktail.

Comments: A favourite at Melbourne's Collins Street exclusive 5 star cocktail bars. Accompanying chocolates make this cocktail bliss before the theatre.

Tropical Itch

Ingredients

Glass: 425mL/14 oz Hurricane Glass

Mixers: 45mL/1 1/2 oz Rum
45mL/1 1/2 oz Bourbon
juice of half fresh lime
dash Angostura Bitters
top-up with pineapple juice and passionfruit
30mL/1 oz Rum, floated

Method

Build over ice.

Garnish: Pineapple spear, mint and cherry plus wooden backscratcher and straws.

Comments: When you're troubled with an itching-tickling throat, delight in this spectacularly garnished fruity cocktail. A proven quenching recipe after sunbaking. The name is derived from the inclusion of the backscratcher.

Voodoo Child

Ingredients

Glass: 90mL/3 oz Cocktail Glass

Mixers: 15mL/1/2 oz Melon Liqueur
15mL/1/2 oz Black Sambuca
15mL/1/2 oz Baileys Irish Cream
15mL/1/2 oz Tia Maria
15mL/1/2 oz Cream

Method

Layer Melon Liqueur on Black Sambuca in glass. Shake other ingredients with ice and strain.

Garnish: Green and black jelly babies on a skewer, then place across top of glass.

Comments: Scare yourself with this novel cocktail. It's a fun filled cocktail guaranteed to lift any spell.

Whisky Sour

Ingredients
Glass: 140mL/5 oz Wine Glass
Mixers: 45mL/1½ oz Scotch Whisky
30mL/1 oz Lemon Juice
15mL/½ oz Sugar syrup
½ Egg white

Method
Shake with ice and strain.
Garnish: Red cherry at bottom of glass and slice of lemon on side.
Comment: A quaint appetiser before dinner. Shake vigorously so the egg white rises to a frothy head after straining. Some people prefer a 140mL/5 oz Cocktail glass.

White Lady

Ingredients
Glass: 90mL/3 oz Cocktail Glass
Mixers: 30mL/1 oz Dry Gin
15mL/½ oz Lemon Juice
15mL/½ oz Sugar Syrup
½ Egg White

Method
Shake with ice and strain.
Garnish: Twist of lemon.
Comments: a traditional pre-dinner cocktail. Pure yet bland, change to either:
"Blue Lady" - substitute Blue Curacao for sugar syrup.
"Pink Lady" - substitute Grenadine for sugar syrup and add cream.

X.T.C.

Ingredients

Glass: 90mL/3 oz Cocktail Glass

Mixers: 30mL/1 oz Tia Maria
30mL/1 oz Strawberry Liqueur
30mL/1 oz Cream

Method

Shake with ice and strain.

Garnish: Butterfly strawberry placed on side of glass, twirl thickened cream over strawberry and sprinkle over flaked chocolate.

Comments: X-rated, tall and cute! Enjoy a truly enjoyable Ecstasy before you dance all night long.

Zombie

Ingredients

Glass: 300mL/10 oz Fancy Cocktail Glass

Mixers: 40mL/1 1/3 oz Bacardi*
30mL/1 oz Dark Rum
30mL/1 oz Light Rum
30mL/1 oz Pineapple Juice
15mL/1/2 oz Lime or Lemon Juice
30mL/1 oz Apricot Brandy
1 teaspoon Sugar Syrup

Method

Shake with ice and pour.

Garnish: Pineapple spear and leaves, cherry and mint leaves, swizzle stick and straws.

Comments: A well-known Hawaiian cocktail. Resurrect yourself with this supernatural Rum-A-Thon cocktail. It is usually the last recipe on cocktail lists.

After Eight

Ingredients
Glass: Cordial (Embassy)
Mixers: 10mL/⅓ oz Kahlúa
10mL/⅓ oz Creme de Menthe
20mL/⅔ oz Baileys Irish Cream
15mL/½ oz Southern Comfort

Method
Pour in order.
Technique: Shoot
Comments: A peppermint surprise.

Atomic Bomb

Ingredients
Glass: Tall Dutch Cordial
Mixers: 20mL/⅔ oz Tia Maria
15mL/½ oz Gin
10mL/⅓ oz Cream

Method
Layer in order, then float cream.
Technique: Shoot
Comments: A strategic 'one shooter weapon', this drink explodes down the unsuspecting throat. Delicious in emergencies! Gin may be replaced with Cointreau, or Triple Sec.

B&B Shooter

Ingredients
Glass: Cordial (Lexington)
Mixers: One part Cognac or Brandy
One part DOM Benedictine

Method
Pour in order.
Technique: Shoot.
Comments: For mature drinkers! Grandpa can turn up the pace of his medication. The shooter is quick and smooth, the traditional B & B cocktail is normally served in a brandy balloon.

Banana Split

Ingredients
Glass: Tall Dutch Cordial
Mixers: 15mL/$1/2$ oz Kahlúa
15mL/$1/2$ oz Lena Banana Liqueur
10mL/$1/3$ oz Strawberry Liqueur
Whipped Cream

Method
Layer in order and top with whipped cream.
Technique: Shoot
Comments: Let this one slip down sweetly, with a super strawberry aftertaste.

Bee Sting

Ingredients
Glass: Cordial (Embassy)
Mixers: 20mL/²/₃ oz Tequila
            10mL/¹/₃ oz Yellow Chartreuse

Method
Layer in order, then light.
Technique: Straw shoot while flaming.
Comments: Ouch! The Yellow Chartreuese attacks your throat with a numbing, pleasurable pain, as Tequila buzzes you back to the party. Drink quickly so the straw won't melt!

Black Nuts

Ingredients
Glass: Cordial (Embassy)
Mixers: 15mL/¹/₂ oz Black Sambucca
            15mL/¹/₂ oz Frangelico

Method
Layer in order.
Technique: Shoot.
Comments: A wonderful "nutty" flavour, with a real anise touch.

Black Widow

Ingredients
Glass: Cordial (Embassy)
Mixers: 10mL/¹/₃ oz Strawberry Liqueur
                10mL/¹/₃ oz Black Sambuca
                10mL/¹/₃ oz Cream

Method
Layer in order.
Technique: Shoot
Comments: Watch this one, the spider will get you quickly.

Blood Bath

Ingredients
Glass: Whisky Shot
Mixers: 10mL/¹/₃ oz Rosso Vermouth
                15mL/¹/₃ oz Strawberry Liqueur
                20mL/²/₃ oz Tequila

Method
Pour in order then layer the Tequila.
Technique: Shoot.
Comments: Cherry grins and rosy cheeks characterise the after effects of this blood thirsty experience. Only issued after midnight and before dawn.

Blow Job

Ingredients
Glass: Cordial (Lexington)
Mixers: Two parts Kahlúa
One part Baileys Irish Cream

Method
Layer in order and shoot.
Technique: Shoot
Comments: A light minty confectionery flavour and creamy texture provide a mouthful for those who indulge. Twist this to a **"Rattlesnake"** by adding Green Chartreuse.

Brain Damage

Ingredients
Glass: Cordial (Embassy)
Mixers: 20mL/^{2}/$_3$ oz Coconut Liqueur
10mL/^{1}/$_3$ oz Parfait Amour Liqueur
5mL/^{1}/$_6$ oz Advocaat Liqueur

Method
Layer the Parfait Amour and Coconut Liqueur, then pour the Advocaat.
Technique: Shoot.
Comments: Separation induces restless nights. Advocaat intervenes to mould the senses.

Brave Bull

Ingredients
Glass: Whiskey Shot
Mixers: 30mL/1 oz Crème de Café Liqueur
15mL/¹/² oz Tequila

Method
Layer in order.
Technique: Shoot
Comments: One of my favourites for late night revellers, will resist fatigue and maintain stamina. Ad Ouzo and a "TKO" is punched out.

Candy Cane

Ingredients
Glass: Tall Dutch Cordial
Mixers: 15mL/¹/² oz Grenadine Cordial
15mL/¹/² oz Creme de Menthe
25mL/⁵/₆ oz Vodka

Method
Layer in order and shoot.
Technique: Shoot
Comments: A real candy flavour, with a touch of menthol.

Chastity Belt

Ingredients
Glass: Tall Dutch Cordial
Mixers: 20mL/²/₃ oz Tia Maria
10mL/¹/₃ oz Frangelico
10mL/¹/₃ oz Baileys Irish Cream
1 teaspoon Cream

Method
Layer in order, then float the cream.
Technique: Shoot
Comments: Morality implores you not to succumb to the super-sweet delicacies of drinking's perversity.

Chilli Shot

Ingredients
Glass: Whisky Shot
Mixers: 45mL/1¹/₂ oz Vodka
Slice of red chilli pepper

Method
Pour.
Technique: Shoot.
Comments: Feeling mischievous? Refrigerate the Vodka with one red chilli pepper (or 3 to 5 drops of Tabasco sauce) for 24 hours before serving.

Chocolate Nougat

Ingredients
Glass: Cordial (Lexington)
Mixers: 10mL/¹/₃ oz Frangelico Hazelnut Liqueur
10mL/¹/₃ oz DOM Benedictine
10mL/¹/₃ oz Baileys Irish Cream

Method
Pour in order then layer the Bailey's Irish Cream.

Technique: Shoot

Comments: A swirling pleasure zone of flowing Bailey's Irish Cream, above the finest Benedictine and based with voluptuous hazelnuts, accentuating the meaning of chocolate.

Coathanger

Ingredients
Glass: Cordial (Lexington)
Mixers: 15mL/¹/₂ oz Cointreau*
15mL/¹/₂ oz Tequila
7mL/¹/₄ oz Grenadine cordial
drop of milk

Method
Layer Tequila onto the Cointreau, dash Cordial or Grenadine then drop the milk.

Technique: Shoot, then cup hand entirely over the rim, insert straw between fingers into the glass and inhale fumes.

Comments: A euphoric experience, quiet stunning to your senses.

* Cointreau may be replaced with Triple Sec Liqueur.

Courting Penelope

Ingredients
Glass: Cordial (Lexington)
Mixers: 20mL/²/₃ oz Cognac
15mL/¹/₂ oz Grand Marnier

Method
Pour in order
Technique: Shoot.
Comments: A distinctive acquired taste is needed for two inseparable moments!

Dark Sunset

Ingredients
Glass: Tall Dutch Cordial
Mixers: One part Dark Crème de Cacao Liqueur
One part Malibu

Method
Layer in order.
Technique: Shoot.
Comments: This tropical paradise reflects sunset, beaches and the ripe coconuts of Malibu.

Devil's Handbrake

Ingredients
Glass: Tall Dutch Cordial
Mixers: 15mL/¹/₂ oz Banana Liqueur
               15mL/¹/₂ oz Mango Liqueur
               15mL/¹/₂ oz Cherry Brandy

Method
Layer in order.

Technique: Shoot

Comments: A magnificent bounty off fruit infiltrated by the devil. Exquisite after a swim.

Dirty Orgasm

Ingredients
Glass: Tall Dutch Cordial
Mixers: 15mL/¹/₂ oz Triple Sec Liqueur
               15mL/¹/₂ oz Galliano
               15mL/¹/₂ oz Baileys Irish Cream

Method
Layer in order.

Technique: Shoot.

Comments: The Irish frolic between the world's two best lovers, Italian Galliano and French Cointreau. Also known as a **"Screaming Orgasm"**. Drambuie may replace Galliano.

Double Date

Ingredients
Glass: Tall Dutch Cordial
Mixers: 15mL/¹/₂ oz Melon Liqueur
              15mL/¹/₂ oz White Crème de Menthe
              15mL/¹/₂ oz DOM Benedictine

Method
Layer in order.
Technique: Tandem.
Comments: Soothing Crème de Menthe restrains the passion of DOM and Melon. For romantics.

Face Off

Ingredients
Glass: Tall Dutch Cordial
Mixers: 10mL/¹/₃ oz Grenadine
              15mL/¹/₂ oz Creme de Menthe
              10mL/¹/₃ oz Parfait Amour
              10mL/¹/₃ oz Sambuca

Method
Layer in order.
Technique: Shoot
Comments: Too many of these will certainly cause a loss of face.

Fizzy Rush

Ingredients

Glass: Tall Dutch Cordial

Mixers: 1 teaspoon White Crème de Menthe

10mL/¹⁄₃ oz Apricot Brandy

30mL/1 oz Champagne

Method

Pour in order.

Technique: Shoot.

Comments: Bubbles of refreshing Apricot guaranteed to get up your nose.

Flaming Lamborghini Shooter

Ingredients

Glass: Cordial (Embassy)

Mixers: 10mL/¹⁄₃ oz Crème de Café Liqueur

10mL/¹⁄₃ oz Galliano

10mL/¹⁄₃ oz Green Chartreuse

Method

Layer in order, then light.

Technique: Shoot while flaming.

Comments: Get the party into motion. Essential for birthday celebrants.

Flaming Lover

Ingredients

Glass: Cordial (Embassy)
Mixers: 15mL/¹/₂ oz Sambuca
               15mL/¹/₂ oz Triple Sec Liqueur

Method

Pour Triple Sec over lit Sambuca while drinking through a straw.
Technique: Straw shoot while flaming.
Comments: The Triple Sec softens the flame for inexperienced drinkers of flaming shooters.

Flaming Orgy

Ingredients

Glass: Tall Dutch Cordial
Mixers: 10mL/¹/₃ oz Grenadine
               10mL/¹/₃ oz Creme de Menthe
               15mL/¹/₂ oz Brandy
               10mL/¹/₃ oz Tequila

Method

Technique: Straw shoot while flaming.
Comments: Another of the potent flaming shooters. Don't get your lips too close to this one.

Flaming Sambuca

Ingredients

Glass: Cordial (Embassy)

Mixers: 30mL/1 oz Sambuca

3 Coffee Beans

Method

Pour Sambuca, float coffee beans and light.

Technique: Shoot after flame extinguished.

Comments: Provides relief from the cold winter. The other way we do it, is to pour Sambuca into a sine glass then light. Cup your hand entirely over the rim while it flames, creating suction. Shake the glass, place under your nose, take your hand from the glass to inhale the fumes, then shoot!

Freddie Fud Pucker

Ingredients

Glass: Cordial (Lexington)

Mixers: 20mL/²⁄₃ oz Galliano

10mL/¹⁄₃ oz Tequila

1 teaspoon Orange Curacao Liqueur

Method

Layer Tequila onto Galliano then drop Orange Curacao.

Technique: Shoot.

Comments: Known to induce dancing on bars and at beach parties, be sure to mind you 'p's and f's' when ordering.

Fruit Tingle

Ingredients
Glass: Cordial (Embassy)
Mixers: 10mL/⅓ oz Blue Curacao Liqueur
15mL/½ oz Mango Liqueur
1 teaspoon Lemon Juice

Method
Layer in order, optional to stir.
Technique: Shoot.
Comments: Tangy and piquant. Melon Liqueur may be substituted for Mango Liqueur.

Galliano Hot Shot

Ingredients
Glass: Galliano Shot Glass
Mixers: 15mL/½ oz Galliano
30mL/1 oz Black Coffee
1 teaspoon Cream

Method
Top Galliano with black coffee, then float cream.
Technique: Shoot.
Comments: When in a hurry, a great way to enjoy a liqueur coffee.

Golden Cadillac Shooter

Ingredients
Glass: Tall Dutch Cordial
Mixers: 15mL/¹/₂ oz White Crème de Cacao
20mL/²/₃ oz Galliano
10mL/¹/₃ oz Cream

Method
Layer Galliano and White Crème de Cacao, then float cream.

Technique: Shoot.

Comments: Comfort in style is what the distilled cocoa beams give golden Galliano - a real dazzler! The traditional Golden Cadillac cocktail has a larger volume, is shaken over ice and served in a 140ml Champagne Saucer.

Grand Slam

Ingredients
Glass: Cordial (Embassy)
Mixers: 10mL/¹/₃ oz Lena Banana Liqueur
10mL/¹/₃ oz Baileys Irish Cream
10mL/¹/₃ oz Grand Marnier

Method
Pour in order, then stir.

Technique: Shoot

Comments: Add more egg white for greater slime. Melon will keep the taste buds occupied, Vodka dilutes the egg white.

Green Slime

Ingredients
Glass: Whiskey Shot
Mixers: 20mL/^{2}/$_3$ oz Melon Liqueur
               15mL/^{1}/$_2$ oz Vodka
               1 teaspoon Egg White

Method
Pour in order, then stir.
Technique: Shoot.
Comments: Add more egg white for greater slime.
Melon will keep the taste buds occupied, Vodka dilutes the egg white.

Half Nelson

Ingredients
Glass: Whiskey Shot
Mixers: 15mL/^{1}/$_2$ oz Crème de Menthe Liqueur
               10mL/^{1}/$_3$ oz Strawberry Liqueur
               20mL/^{2}/$_3$ oz Grand Marnier

Method
Layer in order.
Technique: Shoot.
Comments: The referee is unable to break the grip of Strawberry locking its green opponent into an immovable position. For the temporarily incapacitated.

Harbour Lights

Ingredients

Glass: Cordial (Lexington)

Mixers: 10mL/¹⁄₃ oz Kahlúa

10mL/¹⁄₃ oz Sambuca

10mL/¹⁄₃ oz Green Chartreuse

Method

Layer in order.

Technique: Straw shoot.

Comments: Glittering reflections sparkle on the harbour beside a candlelight dinner. Substitute Yellow Chartreuse if preferred.

Hard On

Ingredients

Glass: Cordial (Embassy)

Mixers: 20mL/²⁄₃ oz Creme de Cafe Liqueur

15mL/¹⁄₂ oz Banana Liqueur

10mL/¹⁄₃ oz Cream

Method

Layer Liqueur onto Kahlua, then float the cream.

Technique: Shoot

Comments: The first to float cream, voted the most popular shooter.

Hellraiser

Ingredients
Glass: Whisky Shot
Mixers: 15mL/¹/₂ oz Strawberry Liqueur
              15mL/¹/₂ oz Melon Liqueur
              15mL/¹/₂ oz Black Sambuca

Method
Layer in order.
Technique: Shoot
Comments: A hell of a drink!

High and Dry

Ingredients
Glass: Cordial (Embassy)
Mixers: 10mL/¹/₃ oz Bianco Vermouth
              15mL/¹/₂ oz Tequila
              1 teaspoon Dry Vermouth

Method
Pour in order, then stir.
Technique: Shoot.
Comments: Disguise the mischief of Tequila with Dry Vermouth. Best served chilled.

Inkahlúarable

Ingredients
Glass: Cordial (Embassy)
Mixers: 10mL/¹/₃ oz Kahlua
10mL/¹/₃ oz Triple Sec Liqueur
10mL/¹/₃ oz Grand Marnier

Method
Layer in order.
Technique: Shoot.
Comments: Terminal illness can be momentarily postponed with this Kahlua-based antidote.

Irish Flag

Ingredients
Glass: Cordial (Lexington)
Mixers: 12mL/¹/₃ oz Green Creme de Menthe
12mL/¹/₃ oz Baileys Irish Cream
12mL/¹/₃ oz Brandy

Method
Layer in order.
Technique: Shoot
Comments: A stroll through verdant pastures. Brandy may be replaced with Tullamore Dew-an Old Irish Whisky.

Italian Stallion

Ingredients
Glass: Cordial (Lexington)
Mixers: 15mL/¹/₂ oz Banana Liqueur
15mL/¹/₂ oz Galliano
1 teaspoon Cream

Method
Pour Galliano onto Banana Liqueur, then float cream. Optional to stir.
Technique: Shoot
Comments: This creamy banana ride you won't forget.

Japanese Slipper

Ingredients
Glass: Tall Dutch Cordial
Mixers: 20mL/²/₃ oz Melon Liqueur
15mL/¹/₂ oz Triple Sec Liqueur*
10mL/¹/₃ oz Lemon Juice

Method
Layer Triple Sec onto the Melon then float the Lemon Juice. Optional to stir.
Technique: Shoot.
Comments: Elegant and refreshing. Precision is required with measurements. To revive failing confidence and replenish that special feeling.

*Cointreau may be substituted for Triple Sec.

Jawbreaker

Ingredients
Glass: Whisky Shot
Mixers: 45mL/1½ oz Apricot Brandy
                  4-5 drops Tabasco Sauce

Method
Pour Apricot Brandy then drop Tabasco Sauce.
Technique: Shoot.
Comments: grit your teeth after this shot, then slowly open your mouth.

Jellyfish

Ingredients
Glass: Cordial (Lexington)
Mixers: 10mL/⅓ oz Blue Curacao Liqueur
                  10mL/⅓ oz Romana Sambuca
                  10mL/⅓ oz Baileys Irish Cream
                  2 dashes of Grenadine

Method
Layer in order and pour Grenadine.
Technique: Shoot.
Comments: Watch out for sting at the end of this slippery shooter.

Jumping Jack Flash

Ingredients
Glass: Whisky Shot
Mixers: 15mL/¹/₂ oz Tia Maria
                15mL/¹/₂ oz Rum
                15mL/¹/₂ oz Jack Daniel's

Method
Layer in order.
Technique: Shoot.
Comments: Thrill seeking Jack Daniel's and his accomplices await this opportunity to shudder your soul.

Jumping Mexican

Ingredients
Glass: Whisky Shot
Mixers: 20mL/²/₃ oz Crème de Café Liqueur
                20mL/²/₃ oz Bourbon

Method
Layer in order.
Technique: Shoot
Comments: Jump into Mexico's favourite pastime and bounce back into the party. For those keen on the Mexican Hat Dance.

Kamikaze Shooter

Ingredients
Glass: Whisky Shot
Mixers: 20mL/²/₃ oz Vodka
15mL/¹/₂ oz Cointreau
10mL/¹/₃ oz Lemon Juice

Method
Layer the Cointreau onto Vodka, float the lemon juice, then optional to stir.

Technique: Shoot

Comments: *Maintain freshness for large volumes by adding strained egg white. Mix in a jug and keep refrigerated. The traditional Kamikaze cocktail has the additional of Lime cordial, it is shaken over ice, strained and then served in a 140ml Cocktail Glass.*

▪Triple Sec may be substituted for Cointreau.

K.G.B. Shooter

Ingredients
Glass: Cordial (Lexington)
Mixers: 10mL/¹/₃ oz Kahlua
10mL/¹/₃ oz Grand Marnier
10mL/¹/₃ oz Baileys Irish Cream

Method
Layer in order.

Technique: Shoot.

Comments: *Grand Marnier adds an orange twist to the Kahlua and Baileys Irish Cream. The traditional K.G.B. cocktail is built over ice with greater volume of ingredient. It is normally served in a 140mL/5 oz Old Fashioned Spirit Glass.*

Kool Aid

Ingredients
Glass: Cordial (Lexington)
Mixers: 10mL/¹/₃ oz Melon Liqueur
15mL/¹/₂ oz Amaretto di Saroono
10mL/¹/₃ oz Vodka

Method
Layer in order.
Technique: Shoot.
Comments: A familiar mix with various names. Amaretto's caramel lacing prevents overheating.

Lady Throat Killer

Ingredients
Glass: Tall Dutch Cordial
Mixers: 20mL/²/₃ oz Crème de Café Liqueur
15mL/¹/₂ oz Melon Liqueur
10mL/¹/₃ oz Frangelico Hazelnut Liqueur

Method
Layer in order.
Technique: Shoot.
Comments: This superb mixture offers an exquisite after-taste. One of my favourite Shooters.

Lambada

Ingredients
Glass: Whisky Shot
Mixers: 15mL/$^1/_2$ oz Mango Liqueur
                15mL/$^1/_2$ oz Black Sambuca
                15mL/$^1/_2$ oz Tequila

Method
Layer in order.
Technique: Shoot.
Comments: *Wiggle your way to the bar and order the latest liqueur, Black Sambuca. Both the dance and the Shooter will excite your partner.*

Laser Beam

Ingredients
Glass: Tall Dutch Cordial
Mixers: 30mL/1 oz Galliano
                20m/$^2/_3$ oz Tequila

Method
Layer in order and shoot.
Technique: Shoot
Comments: *Your palate is illuminated on this celestial journey!*

Lick Sip Suck

Ingredients
Glass: Whisky Shot
Mixers: 30mL/1 oz Tequila
               lemon in quarters or slices
               salt

Method
Pour Tequila into glass. On the flat piece of skin between the base of your thumb and index finger, place a pinch of salt. Place a quarter of the lemon by you on the bar. Lick the salt off your hand, shoot the Tequila and then suck the lemon in quick succession.

Marc's Rainbow

Ingredients
Glass: Whisky Shot
Mixers: 8mL/^{1}/$_5$ oz Crème de Café Liqueur
               8mL/^{1}/$_5$ oz Melon Liqueur
               8mL/^{1}/$_5$ oz Malibu
               8mL/^{1}/$_5$ oz Banana Liqueur
               8mL/^{1}/$_5$ oz Galliano
               8mL/^{1}/$_5$ oz Grand Marnier

Method
Layer in order.
Technique: Shoot.
Comments: One of Melbourne's best shooter recipes. Discover the pot of gold at the end of the rainbow.

Margarita Shooter

Ingredients
Glass: Whisky Shot
Mixers: 15mL/¹/₂ oz Cointreau*
             15mL/¹/₂ oz Tequila
             10mL/¹/₃ oz Lemon Juice
             1 teaspoon Lime Juice

Method
Layer Tequila onto Cointreau, float lemon juice then dash the lime juice.
Technique: Shoot.
Comments: Everyone should take this plunge. Lemon and Lime neutralise the acid. This Shooter is similar to the traditional Margarita cocktail, which is of greater volume, shaken over ice and served in a salt rimmed Champagne Saucer.

*Triple Sec may be substituted for Cointreau.

Martian Hard On

Ingredients
Glass: Tall Dutch Cordial
Mixers: 15mL/¹/₂ oz Dark Crème de Cacao
             15mL/¹/₂ oz Melon Liqueur
             15mL/¹/₂ oz Baileys Irish Cream

Method
Layer in order.
Technique: Shoot.
Comments: When you are a little green about the facts of life.

Melon Splice

Ingredients
Glass: Tall Dutch Cordial
Mixers: 15mL/$^1/_2$ oz Melon Liqueur
15mL/$^1/_2$ oz Galliano
15mL/$^1/_2$ oz Coconut Liqueur

Method
Layer in order.
Technique: Shoot.
Comments: Synonymous with Sunday strolls and ice-cream. Flakes of ice may be sprinkled to chill.

Mexican Flag

Ingredients
Glass: Tall Dutch Cordial
Mixers: 15mL/$^1/_2$ oz Grenadine Cordial
15mL/$^1/_2$ oz Creme de Menthe
15mL/$^1/_2$ oz Tequila

Method
Layer in order and shoot.
Technique: Shoot
Comments: Try this "South of the Border" flag waver.

Nude Bomb

Ingredients

Glass: Cordial (Embassy)

Mixers: 10mL/¹/₃ oz Kahlúa
10mL/¹/₃ oz Banana Liqueur
10mL/¹/₃ oz Amaretto di Saronno

Method

Layer in order.

Technique: Shoot

Comments: Especially created for toga-parties and skinny-dipping.

Orgasm Shooter

Ingredients

Glass: Whisky Shot

Mixers: One part Coinreau*
One part Baileys Irish Cream

Method

Layer in order.

Technique: Shoot.

Comments: After the first one, you most certainly will want another. The Shooter method is different to the traditional Orgasm cocktail, which is a linger drink, built over ice and served in a 210ml Old Fashioned Spirit Glass.

*Triple Sec may be substituted for Cointreau.

Oyster Shooter

Ingredients
Glass: Cordial (Embassy)
Mixers: 10mL/$\frac{1}{3}$ oz Vodka
             10mL/$\frac{1}{3}$ oz Tomato Juice
             1 teaspoon Cocktail Sauce (see page 10)
             Worcestershire sauce to taste
             Tabasco sauce to taste
             1 fresh oyster

Method
Pour tomato juice onto the Vodka, float the cocktail sauce, dash sauces to taste and drop in oyster.
Technique: Shoot.
Comments: An early morning wake-up call, replenishing energy lost the night before. Also referred to as a Heart Starter.

Passion Juice

Ingredients
Glass: Whisky Shot
Mixers: 20mL/$\frac{2}{3}$ oz Orange Curacao Liqueur
             10mL/$\frac{1}{3}$ oz Cherry Brandy Liqueur
             15mL/$\frac{1}{2}$ oz freshly squeezed Orange
             or Lemon juice

Method
Layer in order. Optional to stir.
Technique: Shoot.
Comments: A bitter sweet lift by garnishing liqueur passion with juices.

Peach Tree Bay

Ingredients
Glass: Tall Dutch Cordial
Mixers: 30mL/1 oz Peachtree Schnapps
    15m/$\frac{1}{2}$ oz Pimm's No. 1 Cup
    1 teaspoon Crème de Menthe Liqueur

Method
Layer the Pimm's onto the Peachtree Schnapps, then drop Green Crème de Menthe.
Technique: Shoot.
Comments: Conjuring an image of uninhabited places, cool refreshing Pimm's is minted with Green Crème de Menthe.

Peachy Bum

Ingredients
Glass: Tall Dutch Cordial
Mixers: 20mL/$\frac{2}{3}$ oz Mango Liqueur
    15mL/$\frac{1}{2}$ oz Peachtree Schnapps
    10mL/$\frac{1}{3}$ oz Cream

Method
Layer in order.
Technique: Shoot.
Comments: Delightfully enriched and mellowed by fresh cream.

Pearl Necklace

Ingredients
Glass: Cordial (Embassy)
Mixers: 15mL/1/2 oz Melon Liqueur
15mL/1/2 oz Pimm's No. 1 Cup

Method
Layer in order.
Technique: Shoot.
Comments: a dash of lemonade (7-up) dilutes the zappy after-taste.

Perfect Match

Ingredients
Glass: Cordial (Lexington)
Mixers: 20mL/2/3 oz Parfait Amour Liqueur
20mL/2/3 oz Malibu

Method
Layer in order.
Technique: Shoot.
Comments: Parfaits (Perfect), Amour (Love), proposes future happiness and togetherness and under Malibu's exotic veil.

Pipeline

Ingredients
Glass: Tall Dutch Cordial
Mixers: 30mL/1 oz Tequila
                 20mL/^{2}/$_3$ oz Vodka

Method
Layer in order.
Technique: Shoot
Comments: Ride the wild surf in this pipeline.

Pipsqueak

Ingredients
Glass: Cordial (Embassy)
Mixers: 20mL/^{2}/$_3$ oz Frangelico Hazelnut Liqueur
                 10mL/^{1}/$_3$ oz Vodka
                 1 teaspoon Lemon Juice

Method
Layer in order, then stir.
Technique: Shoot.
Comments: Another favourite of mine. A quaint appetiser before dinner.

Rabbit-Punch

Ingredients
Glass: Whisky Shot
Mixers: 10mL/⅓ oz Campari
10mL/⅓ oz Dark Crème de Cacao
10mL/⅓ oz Malibu
15mL/½ oz Baileys Irish Cream

Method
Pour in order then layer Baileys Irish Cream.
Technique: Shoot.
Comments: Baileys Irish Cream assures credibility and its softness will subtly inflict a powerful jab to wake you up and keep you on the hop!

Ready, Set, Go!

Ingredients
Glass: Tall Dutch Cordial
Mixers: 15mL/½ oz Strawberry Liqueur
15mL/½ oz Banana Liqueur
15mL/½ oz Midori

Method
Layer in order and straw shoot.

Red Indian

Ingredients

Glass: Cordial (Lexington)
Mixers: 10mL/¹⁄₃ oz Dark Crème de Cacao
10mL/¹⁄₃ oz Peachtree Schnapps
15mL/¹⁄₂ oz Canadian Club

Method

Layer in order.
Technique: Shoot.
Comments: Dark Crème de Cacao ripens the Peachtree to tantalise. CC takes the scalp!

Rusty Nail

Ingredients

Glass: Cordial (Embassy)
Mixers: 15mL/¹⁄₂ oz Scotch Whisky
15mL/¹⁄₂ oz Drambuie

Method

Layer in order.
Technique: Shoot.
Comments: A pillow-softener, though this age-old blend will never cause fatigue. As a Shooter, great as "one for the road". The traditional cocktail is normally built over ice, in a 210ml Old Fashioned Spirit Glass.

Ryan's Rush

Ingredients

Glass: Cordial (Embassy)
Mixers: 10mL/⅓ oz Kahlúa
                    10mL/⅓ oz Baileys Irish Cream
                    10mL/⅓ oz Rum

Method

Layer in order.

Technique: Shoot

Comments: An easy one. Don't be lulled by the pleasant taste, this one has a real kick.

Screaming Death Shooter

Ingredients

Glass: Tall Dutch Cordial
Mixers: 15mL/½ oz Crème de Café Liqueur
                    10mL/⅓ oz Cougar Bourbon
                    10mL/⅓ oz DOM Benedictine
                    1 teaspoon Bourbon
                    1 teaspoon Dark Rum OP

Method

Layer in the above order. Lighting optional.

Technique: Shoot while flaming.

Comments: The pinnacle of endurance. Double layers of flammable fuel cushioned in ascending order by Crème de Café Liqueur, Bourbon and Benedictine, which sweetly numbs any pain. It's truth and dare.

Screwdriver Shooter

Ingredients
Glass: Whisky Shot
Mixers: 15mL/½ oz Orange Liqueur
30mL/1½ oz Vodka

Method
Layer in order.
Technique: Shoot.
Comments: Add a dash of Peachtree Schnapps and it's known as a "Fuzzy Navel". The Shooter mix departs from the traditional Screwdriver cocktail by the substitution of Orange Liqueur for Orange juice. The cocktail is also built over ice in a 210ml Old Fashioned Spirit glass.

Sex in the Snow

Ingredients
Glass: Cordial (Lexington)
Mixers: 12mL/⅓ oz Triple Sec Liqueur
12mL/⅓ oz Malibu
12mL/⅓ oz Ouzo

Method
Pour in order, then stir.
Technique: Straw Shoot.
Comments: the sub-zero temperature of this combination is chillingly refreshing when drunk through a straw.

Sherbert Burp

Ingredients
Glass: Tall Dutch Cordial
Mixers: 15mL/½ oz Strawberry Liqueur
             30mL/1 oz Champagne

Method
Pour Strawberry Liqueur then top up with Champagne.
Technique: Shoot.
Comments: Change the colour of your burp with any flavoured liqueur. Even better, multi-colour it!

Sidecar Shooter

Ingredients
Glass: Cordial (Lexington)
Mixers: 10mL/⅓ oz Brandy
             15mL/½ oz Cointreau*
             10mL/⅓ oz Lemon Juice

Method
Layer Cointreau onto Brandy, float Lemon Juice, then optional to stir.
Technique: Shoot.
Comments: This old-fashioned, lemon-barley refreshment, filtered through Cointreau and lightly tanned with Brandy, restores your zest for life. A slightly different mix to the traditional Sidecar cocktail, which is shaken over ice and served in a 90ml Cocktail glass.

*Cointreau may be substituted with Triple Sec.

Silver Thread

Ingredients
Glass: Tall Dutch Cordial
Mixers: 15mL/¹/₂ oz Creme de Menthe
             15mL/¹/₂ oz Banana Liqueur
             15mL/¹/₂ oz Tia Maria

Method
Layer in order.
Technique: Shoot or lick, sip and suck.
Comments: A great shooter to mend the fences. Try this one on with the oldies.

Slippery Nipple

Ingredients
Glass: Cordial (Embassy)
Mixers: 30mL/1 oz Sambuca
             15mL/¹/₂ oz Baileys Irish Cream

Method
Layer in order.
Technique: Shoot
Comments: One of the originals, very well received. Cream floated on the Baileys becomes a **"Pregnant Slippery Nipple".** Grand Marnier included makes a **"Slipadicthome".**

Snake Bite

Ingredients

Glass: Cordial (Embassy)
Mixers: 20mL/$^2/_3$ oz Creme de Cafe Liqueur
10mL/$^1/_3$ oz Green Chartreuse

Method

Layer in order, then light.
Technique: Straw shoot while flaming.
Comments: Score this shooter ten out of ten. Drink quickly or the straw will melt.

Spanish Fly

Ingredients

Glass: Whisky Shot
Mixers: 10mL/$^1/_3$ oz Bianco Vermouth
15mL/$^1/_2$ oz Tequila
20mL/$^2/_3$ oz Whisky

Method

<<<<<<<<<No Method>>>>>>>>>>>>>>>>
Technique: Tandem.
Comments: No, it's not what you're twinkling eye and devious smirk assumes...it's better. A guaranteed survival capsule, capable of producing fantasies beyond those Spain is famous for.

Springbok

Ingredients
Glass: Cordial (Embassy)
Mixers: 20mL/²/₃ oz Passionfruit Syrup
10mL/¹/₃ oz Crème de Menthe Liqueur
1 teaspoon Ouzo

Method
Layer in order.
Technique: Shoot.
Comments: Named after the beautiful Springbok of Africa, formerly a motif on the South African Rugby jersey.

Strawberry Cream

Ingredients
Glass: Cordial (Embassy)
Mixers: 20mL/²/₃ oz Strawberry Liqueur
10mL/¹/₃ oz Cream

Method
Layer in order.
Technique: Shoot.
Comments: begin your trip to the "World of Shooters" with this one. Cream acts as a buffer to entice the nervous and inexperienced. Strawberries calm what was needless concern.

Suction Cup

Ingredients
Glass: Cordial (Lexington)
Mixers: 20mL/^{2}/$_3$ oz Vodka
           10mL/^{1}/$_3$ oz Melon Liqueur
           1 teaspoon Blue Curacao Liqueur

Method
Layer the Melon onto Vodka, then pour Blue Curacao.
Technique: Suction-straw shoot.
Comments: A supersonic vacuum results from this drinking method.

Suitor

Ingredients
Glass: Cordial (Lexington)
Mixers: 10mL/^{1}/$_3$ oz Drambuie*
           10mL/^{1}/$_3$ oz Grand Marnier
           10mL/^{1}/$_3$ oz Baileys Irish Cream
           1 teaspoon Milk

Method
Pour in order.
Technique: Shoot.
Comments: Milk inclusion coddles a cool moment, resettles anxieties when approaching the fair sex, guaranteed to excite romance.
*Drambuie may be substituted with Lochan Ora.

Sukiyaki

Ingredients
Glass: Cordial (Embassy)
Mixers: 10mL/¹/₃ oz Mango Liqueur
10mL/¹/₃ oz Apricot Brandy
10mL/¹/₃ oz Malibu

Method
Layer in order.
Technique: Shoot.
Comments: Essential starter for s superb Japanese banquet.

Test Tube Baby

Ingredients
Glass: Tall Dutch Cordial
Mixers: 30mL/1 oz Grand Marnier
20mL/²/₃ oz Ouzo
drop of Baileys Irish Cream

Method
Layer in order and shoot.
Technique: Shoot
Comments: Bubbles of refreshing Apricot guaranteed to get up your nose.

The Day After

Ingredients

Glass: Cordial (Embassy)
Mixers: 10mL/¹⁄₃ oz Cointreau*
10mL/¹⁄₃ oz Tequila
5 drops Blue Curacao Liqueur
10mL/¹⁄₃ oz Green Chartreuse

Method

Layer Tequila onto Cointreau. Drop the Blue Curacao, then layer Green Chartreuse and light.

Technique: Shoot after flame extinguished.

Comments: An upside down day!

*Cointreau may be substituted with Triple Sec.

T.K.O.

Ingredients

Glass: Cordial (Embassy)
Mixers: 10mL/¹⁄₃ oz Kahlúa
10mL/¹⁄₃ oz Tequila
10mL/¹⁄₃ oz Ouzo

Method

Layer in order.

Technique: Shoot.

Comments: Don't fall with this TKO, drink it with pleasure, recover without pain.

Tickled Pink

Ingredients
Glass: Whisky shot
Mixers: 45mL/1½ oz White Crème de Menthe
              1 teaspoon Grenadine Cordial

Method
Pour White Crème de Menthe followed by a dash of
Grenadine or Raspberry Cordial.
Technique: Shoot.
Comments: For those who are bashful when
complimented.

Towering Inferno

Ingredients
Glass: Cordial (Embassy)
Mixers: 10mL/⅓ oz Dry Gin
              10mL/⅓ oz Triple Sec Liqueur
              10mL/⅓ oz Green Chartreuse

Method
Layer in order, then light.
Technique: Shoot while flaming.
Comments: Designed to set the night on fire.

Traffic Light

Ingredients
Glass: Tall Dutch Cordial
Mixers: 10mL/¹/₃ oz Strawberry Liqueur
10mL/¹/₃ oz Galliano
30mL/1 oz Green Chartreuse

Method
Layer in order, light, then light.
Technique: Suction-straw shoot.
Comments: Ready set go! Substitute Banana Liqueur for Galliano and Melon Liqueur for Green Chartreuse, for those with a sweet tooth.

U-Turn

Ingredients
Glass: Whisky Shot
Mixers: 15mL/¹/₂ oz Banana Liqueur
30mL/1 oz Tia Maria

Method
Layer in order.
Technique: Shoot.
Comments: The Banana offers the curve yet its Tia Maria that sends you around the bend. A complete change of direction.

Vibrator

Ingredients

Glass: Cordial (Embassy)
Mixers: 10mL/¹/₃ oz Baileys Irish Cream
20mL/²/₃ oz Southern Comfort

Method

Layer in order.
Technique: Shoot.
Comments: Batteries are not required for this stimulating and pulsating comfort.

Violet Slumber

Ingredients

Glass: Cordial (Lexington)
Mixers: 15mL/¹/₂ oz Malibu
10mL/¹/₃ oz Parfait Amour
10mL/¹/₃ oz Orange juice

Method

Layer in order.
Technique: Shoot.
Comments: Pretty to look at, better to drink, but don't slumber on this number.

Vodka-Tini

Ingredients
Glass: Cordial (Embassy)
Mixers: 30mL/1 oz Vodka
1 teaspoon Dry Vermouth

Method
Pour in order, then stir.
Technique: Shoot.
Comments: No olive is required. Preferably served chilled.

Water-Bubba

Ingredients
Glass: Cordial (Embassy)
Mixers: 15mL/½ oz Cherry Advocaat
10mL/⅓ oz Advocaat
10mL/⅓ oz Blue Curacao

Method
Pour Advocaat into Cherry Advocaat, then layer the Blue Curacao and shoot.
Technique: Shoot.
Comments: The Advocaat resembles an egg yolk, with veins of Cherry Advocaat. Also known as an **"Unborn Baby"**.

Andy Williams

Ingredients

Glass: 290mL/9 oz Old Fashioned Glass
Mixers: 60mL/2 oz Claytons Tonic
              15mL/½ oz Lime juice
              dash sugar syrup
              top-up with soda water

Method

Shake with ice and pour

Garnish: Thin lime slice floated in drink.

Comments: A delightful pre-dinner drink.

Andy's Passion

Ingredients

Glass: 270mL/9 oz Hi-Ball Glass
Mixers: 90mL/3 oz Passionfruit pulp
              90mL/3 oz Tropical juice
              60mL/2 oz Natural yoghurt

Method

Blend with ice and pour.

Garnish: Lime slice, swizzle stick and straw.

Comments: A taste of sunshine with the unique tang of passionfruit.

Angel's Kiss

Ingredients

Glass: 290mL/9 oz Poco Grande Glass
Mixers: scoop Vanilla Ice Cream
tablespoon Passionfruit pulp
150mL/5 oz Apricot nectar

Method

Blend with ice and pour.

Garnish: Mint leaves.

Comments: A wonderful blend of passionfruit and apricots.

Apricot Smoothie

Ingredients

Glass: 390mL/12 oz Poco Grande Glass
Mixers: 2 Apricots
90mL/3 oz Milk
15mL/½ oz Lemon juice
30mL/1 oz Vanilla yoghurt

Method

Blend with ice and pour.

Garnish: Apricot slice and straws.

Comments: A large smooth drink, with apricot flavour.

Apricot Supreme

Ingredients
Glass: 270mL/9 oz Hi-Ball Glass
Mixers: 150mL/5 oz Apricot nectar
60mL/2 oz Orange juice
15mL/½ oz Lemon juice

Method
Shake with ice and pour
Garnish: Orange slice, mint leaves and straw.
Comments: The sweet fruit alternative.

Banana Bash

Ingredients
Glass: 310mL/10 oz Hi-Ball Glass
Mixers: 1 ripe Banana
4 Raspberries
scoop Vanilla ice cream
90mL/3 oz Tropical fruit juice

Method
Blend with ice and pour
Garnish: A sugar dusted raspberry on a banana wedge.
Comments: A great tasting blend of raspberry and banana.

Banana Berry Smoothy

Ingredients
Glass:　170mL/6 oz Champagne Flute
Mixers:　$1/3$ ripe Banana
　　　　　60mL/2 oz Orange juice
　　　　　3 tablespoons Mixed berries

Method
Blend with ice and pour.
Garnish: Wedge banana and straw.
Comments: Berry bonanza.

Banana-Choc Shake

Ingredients
Glass:　440mL/14 oz Hurricane Glass
Mixers:　1 ripe banana, sliced
　　　　　2 scoops chocolate ice cream
　　　　　200mL/7 oz milk

Method
Blend with ice and pour.
Garnish: Teaspoon grated chocolate and straw.
Comments: The biggest chocolate milkshake with a faint banana overtone.

Banana Smoothy

Ingredients
Glass: 270mL/9 oz Hi-Ball Glass
Mixers: 120mL/4 oz Orange Juice
1 ripe Banana
30mL/1 oz Sugar syrup
dash lime juice

Method
Blend with ice and pour.
Garnish: Edge glass with banana wedge and lime slice.
Comments: Smooth, healthy and sweet.

Banberry

Ingredients
Glass: 200mL/7 oz Baccus Wine Glass
Mixers: 4 small Strawberries
$1/2$ ripe Banana
90mL/3 oz Milk
30mL/1 oz Sugar syrup

Method
Blend with ice and pour.
Garnish: Small strawberry on rim of glass.
Comments: Thick, creamy, luscious, strawberry drink.

Be Bop A Do Da

Ingredients
Glass: 200mL/6 oz Bacchus Wine Glass
Mixers: ½ ripe banana
tablespoon passionfruit pulp
tablespoon crushed pineapple
15mL/½ oz Lemon juice

Method
Blend with ice and pour.
Garnish: Long pineapple wedge and optional decoration.
Comments: A thick and very tasty, tropical drink.

Bee Sting

Ingredients
Glass: 200mL/6 oz Old Fashioned Glass
Mixers: 90mL/3 oz Apple juice
30mL/1 oz Orange juice
2 teaspoons honey
15mL/½ oz lime juice

Method
Blend with ice and strain.
Garnish: Sugar frosted apple slice.
Comments: Sweet nectar from the bee hive.

Bell's Beach

Ingredients
Glass: 650mL/20 oz Hurricane Glass
Mixers: 100mL/3 oz Orange juice
100mL/3 oz pineapple juice
$^1/_2$ Egg white
top-up with lemonade (7-up)

Method
Shake with ice and pour
Garnish: None.
Comments: A giant fluffy fruit juice.

Bell's Boomer

Ingredients
Glass: 470mL/16 oz Fancy Hi-Ball Glass
Mixers: 30mL/1 oz Apple juice
30mL/1 oz Orange juice
30mL/1 oz Grapefruit juice
30mL/1 oz Lime juice
120mL/4 oz dry ginger ale

Method
Build over Ice.
Garnish:
Comments: A large energising fruit drink, ideal before tackling those early morning breakers.

Ben's Play Lunch

Ingredients

Glass: 330mL/12 oz Hi-Ball Glass

Mixers: 1 ripe Banana
            3 tablespoons crushed pineapple
            60mL/2 oz Coconut cream
            60mL/2 oz Tropical fruit juice
            15mL/½ oz Lemon juice

Method

Blend with ice and pour.

Garnish: Desiccated coconut frosted glass, with optional decoration.

Comments: A thick fruity drink to assist your primate instincts.

Blushing Berry

Ingredients

Glass: 260mL/8 oz Margarita Glass

Mixers: 150mL/5 oz milk
            60mL/2 oz raspberry cordial
            60mL/2 oz cream
            15mL/½ oz coconut milk
            frozen raspberries

Method

Blend with ice, raspberry cordial, coconut milk, milk and whipped cream.

Garnish: Place frozen raspberries around rim.

Comments: Created by Mary Jane Porta of Termo, Albury and was a finalist in the Best Border Beverage Competition.

Bobby Dazzler

Ingredients

Glass: 290mL/9 oz Poco Grande Glass
Mixers: 60mL/2 oz Grenadine
200mL/6 oz Cola
whipped cream
hundreds and thousands

Method

Blend Grenadine with ice and pour.

Garnish: Pour into glass, top with whipped cream and sprinkle with hundreds and thousands. Place strawberry on side and serve with swizzle stick and straw.

Comments: By Maxine Nash, Bubbles-Wodonga Hotel, was a runner-up in the Best Border Beverage Competition.

Bobby's Booze Buster

Ingredients

Glass: 290mL/9 oz Poco Grande Glass
Mixers: ½ Banana
30mL/1 oz Coconut cream
50mL/1²/₃ oz Apple juice
scoop Vanilla ice cream
sprinkle Cinnamon

Method

Blend with ice and pour.

Garnish: Apple wedge and cinnamon stick.

Comments: A very refreshing, slightly bitter-sweet drink.

Brazilian Breakdance

Ingredients

Glass: 390mL/12 oz Poco Grande Glass
Mixers: 2 teaspoons Instant coffee
Scoop Vanilla ice cream
125mL/4 oz Milk

Method

Blend with ice and pour.
Garnish: Teaspoon chocolate flakes.
Comments: A luscious, thick glass of iced coffee flavour, with just a hint of sweetness.

Candy Bar

Ingredients

Glass: 290mL/9 oz Poco Grande Glass
Mixers: 200mL/6 oz Milk
15mL/½ oz Chocolate topping
30mL/1 oz Caramel topping
whipped cream

Method

Blend with ice, milk chocolate and caramel topping.
Garnish: Top with whipped cream and sprinkle with icing sugar and shaved chocolate.
Comments: Created by Mary Ann Macure of Anthony's Restaurant, Wodonga and was a finalist in the Best Border Beverage Competition.

Cane Toad

Ingredients

Glass:	225mL/8 oz Fancy Hi-Ball Glass
Mixers:	30mL/1 oz Passionfruit pulp
	30mL/1 oz Sugar syrup
	30mL/1 oz Lemon juice
	Top-up with Dry ginger ale

Method

Shake with ice and pour.

Garnish: Two lemon slices and mint leaves.

Comments: A fizzy cane toad without the poison, a very refreshing tarty drink.

Carrot Wizz

Ingredients

Glass:	200mL/6oz Old Fashioned Glass
Mixers:	60mL/2 oz Tomato juice
	½ medium carrot (thinly sliced)
	dash horseradish sauce
	dash Lemon juice

Method

Blend with ice and pour.

Garnish: Carrot top, floated on top.

Comments: "What's up Doc?" Created by Blaza Nikolic of the Hyatt Hotel, Melbourne.

Champagne Mocktail

Ingredients
Glass: 260mL/8 oz Tulip Champagne Flute
Mixers: Sugar cube
           30mL/1 oz Apple juice
           125mL/4 oz Lemon-lime mineral water

Method
Build over ice.
Garnish: Optional decoration.
Comments: Cool summer refresher.

Chiquitta

Ingredients
Glass: 200mL/6 oz Baccus Wine Glass
Mixers: 1 ripe Banana, thinly sliced
           60mL/2 oz Orange juice
           15mL/$\frac{1}{2}$ oz Cream
           dash Grenadine

Method
Blend with ice and strain.
Garnish: orange slice with twist.
Comments: The smoothie that drives you bananas.

Chocolate Cream

Ingredients
Glass: 270mL/9 oz Hi-Ball Glass
Mixers: 2 teaspoons Cocoa powder
                90ml/3 oz Milk
                30mL/1 oz Cream
                60mL/2 oz Sugar syrup

Method
Blend with ice and pour.
Garnish: Sprinkle cocoa powder over top.
Comments: The classic chocolate temptation.

Chocolate Frog

Ingredients
Glass: 390mL/12 oz Poco Grande Glass
Mixers: 250mL/8 oz Cola
                15mL/1/2 oz Chocolate topping
                dash Peppermint essence
                Whipping cream

Method
Build over ice.
Garnish: Top with whipped cream and sprinkle with nutmeg and place sliced strawberry on side of glass. Serve with swizzle stick and straw.
Comments: by Annie Brouwer of Thermo-Albury and was a runner-up in the Best Border Beverage Competition.

Chysathemum

Ingredients
Glass: 290mL/9 oz Salud Grande Glass
Mixers: 90mL/3 oz Dark grape juice
Dash Grenadine cordial
45mL/1¹/₂ oz Soda water

Method
Build over ice and stir.
Garnish: None.
Comments: The sharp classic taste of pure grape.

Claytons Sour

Ingredients
Glass: 200mL/6 oz Bacchus Wine Glass
Mixers: 90mL/3 oz Claytons Tonic
15mL/¹/₂ oz Sugar syrup
60mL/2 oz Lemon Juice

Method
Shake with ice and pour.
Garnish: Maraschino cherry.
Comments: Along the traditional lines.

Clover Blossom

Ingredients
Glass: 270mL/9 oz Hi-Ball Glass
Mixers: 60mL/2 oz Lemon Cordial
                30mL/1 oz Lime Juice
                1 Egg White
                dash Grenadine
                Top-up with Tonic Water

Method
Blend with ice and pour.
Garnish: Lemon slice, mint leaf and straw.
Comments: A delicate fluffy concoction.

Cock-A-Doodle

Ingredients
Glass: 290mL/9 oz Salud Grande Glass
Mixers: 90mL/3 oz Dark grape juice
                90mL/3 oz Lemon juice
                15mL/½ oz Lime cordial
                15mL/½ oz Sugar syrup
                dash Grenadine

Method
Shake with ice and strain.
Garnish: Lime slice and dark grapes on side of glass.
Comments: Wake up to this little refresher.

Coco Cream

Ingredients

Glass: 260mL/8 oz Tulip Champagne Flute
Mixers: 80mL/2²/₃ oz Dark grape juice
110mL/3¹/₃ oz Orange juice
30mL/1 oz Coconut cream
15mL/¹/₂ oz Grenadine

Method

Shake with ice and strain

Garnish: Frost glass with desiccated coconut and add maraschino cherry.

Comments: A fruity drink, with coconut influence.

Cocomint

Ingredients

Glass: 270mL/9 oz Hi-Ball Glass
Mixers: Scoop Chocolate ice cream
30mL/1 oz Coconut cream
60mL/2 oz Milk
30mL/1 oz Lime cordial

Method

Blend with ice and pour.

Garnish: Teaspoon crushed peppermint crisp bar, mint leaves.

Comments: A rich creamy coconut-chocolate blend.

Coffee Crunch

Ingredients

Glass: 440mL/14 oz Hurricane Glass
Mixers: 90mL/3 oz Coconut cream
             90mL/3 oz Cream
             1 egg
             125mL/4 oz iced coffee

Method

Blend with ice and pour.

Garnish: Sprinkle with cinnamon sugar, serve with straw and decorate as desired.

Comments: Created by Gaye Fendyke of Termo-Albury and was a runner-up in the Best Border Beverage Competition.

Corio Bay Sunset

Ingredients

Glass: 330mL/11 oz Hi-Ball glass
Mixers: 4 Large Strawberries
             30mL/1 oz Lime juice
             125mL/4 oz Orange and mango juice
             15mL/½ oz Claytons Tonic
             Top-up with Lemonade (7-up)

Method

Blend with ice and strain.

Garnish: Orange slice.

Comments: A delightful combination of citrus and berry flavours.

Corra Bear

Ingredients
Glass: 290mL/10 oz Poco Grande Glass
Mixers: 200mL/6 oz Cola
30mL/1 oz Iced coffee
Whipped cream

Method
Build over ice and stir.
Garnish: Top with whipped cream and place maraschino cherry on top, with a slice of kiwi fruit on side of glass. Serve with straws.
Comments: Created by Mary Jane Porta of Termo, Albury and was outright winner of the Best Border Beverages Competition.

Creamy Banana

Ingredients
Glass: 350mL/12 oz Fiesta Grande Glass
Mixers: 1 ripe Banana, sliced
30mL/1 oz Coconut cream
60mL/2 oz Milk
Scoop Vanilla ice cream

Method
Blend with ice and strain.
Garnish: Sprinkle with chocolate flakes.
Comments: A delicate creamy drink.

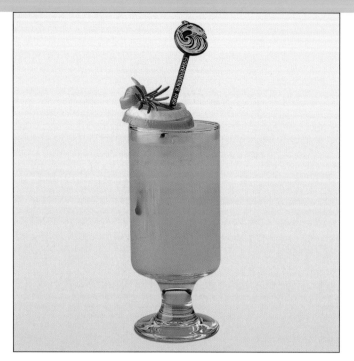

Crocodile

Ingredients
Glass: 270mL/9 oz Footed Hi-Ball Glass
Mixers: 60mL/2 oz Grapefruit juice
30mL/1 oz Lime juice
30mL/1 oz Sugar syrup
Top-up with Lemonade (7-up)

Method
Shake with ice and stir.
Garnish: Lime peel curl.
Comments: A citrus tang makes this drink a perfect summer cooler.

Dark Clouds

Ingredients
Glass: 330mL/10 oz Hi-Ball Glass
Mixers: 125mL/4 oz Cola
60mL/2 oz Claytons Tonic
60mL/2 oz Dry ginger ale

Method
Build over ice.
Garnish: Vanilla bean and swizzle stick.
Comments: An aromatic cooler.

Dick Little

Ingredients
Glass: 350mL/12 oz Fancy Hi-Ball Glass
Mixers; 60mL/2 oz Apricot nectar
15mL/½ oz Lime juice
Top-up with Bitter lemon

Method
Build over ice.
Garnish: Lemon slices on side of glass, swizzle stick and straw.

Doctor's Orders

Ingredients
Glass: 290mL/9 oz Salud Grande Glass
Mixers: 30mL/1 oz Lime juice
125mL/4 oz Grapefruit juice
2 sachets Lite-n-Low
Top-up with Tonic Water

Method
Shake with ice and strain.
Garnish: Lime slice and straws.
Comments: A juice a day to keep the doctor away.

Dust Settler

Ingredients
Glass: 290mL/9 oz Poco Grande Glass
Mixers: 90mL/3 oz Crushed pineapple
              90mL/3 oz Apple juice
              Top-up with Lemonade (7-up)

Method
Blend with ice and pour.

Garnish: Apple slice

Comments: Sweet and smooth, guaranteed to settle the dust.

Frenzee

Ingredients
Glass: 380mL/12 oz Viva Grande Glass
Mixers: 3 large Strawberries
              Sachet Lite-n-Low
              60mL/2 oz Pineapple yoghurt
              60mL/2 oz Pineapple juice
              Top-up with Soda water

Method
Blend with ice and pour.

Garnish: Punch straw through strawberry and sit it in the glass.

Comments: Tropical dairy delight.

Fruit Mocquiri

Ingredients
Glass: 260mL/8 oz Margarita Glass
Mixers: 60mL/2 oz Strawberries, peaches or mango
15mL/$^1/_2$ oz Sugar syrup
15mL/$^1/_2$ oz Lemon juice
30mL/1 oz Apple juice

Method
Blend with ice and pour.
Garnish: Small slice of the ingredient fruit.
Comments: A smooth rich blend of your favourite fruit. I particularly like mango, as used in the photograph above.

Fruit Squash

Ingredients
Glass: 330mL/10 oz Hi-Ball Glass
Mixers: 2 Strawberries
4 Raspberries
tablespoon crushed pineapple
tablespoon Passionfruit pulp
$^1/_2$ Kiwi fruit
60mL/2 oz Orange juice

Method
Blend with ice and pour.
Garnish: Berry studded pineapple spear.
Comments: A fruit lovers delight.

Gator

Ingredients
Glass: 170mL/6 oz Champagne Flute
Mixers: 90mL/3 oz Grapefruit juice
              30mL/1 oz Lime cordial

Method
Build over ice.
Garnish: Lime peel curl.
Comments: Sharp and tangy aperitif.

Ginger Mick

Ingredients
Glass: 290mL/9 oz Old Fashioned Glass
Mixers: 125mL/4 oz Dry ginger ale
              15mL/½ oz Lime juice
              30mL/1 oz Claytons Tonic
              30mL/1 oz Lemon juice
              60mL/2 oz Apple juice

Method
Stir with ice.

Garnish: Apple peel threaded inside glass, with lemon slice on side with mint sprig.

Comments: A thirst quenching drink to combat the summer sun.

Health Farm

Ingredients

Glass: 270mL/9 oz Hi-Ball Glass
Mixers: 90mL/3 oz Pineapple juice
2 slices Cantaloupe melon
90mL/3 oz Orange juice
2 teaspoons Honey
$1/2$ ripe Banana

Method

Blend with ice and pour.
Garnish: Cantaloupe wedge and swizzle stick.
Comments: A great drink for the health conscious.
Created by Wayne Baker or Tousson Restaurant, Geelong.

Henry VIII

Ingredients

Glass: 210mL/7 oz Old Fashioned Glass
Mixers: 60mL/2 oz Apple juice
15mL/$1/2$ oz Lemon juice
Top-up with Dry Ginger Ale
$1/2$ teaspoon of Grenadine

Method

Build over ice.
Garnish: To finish, gently add Grenadine to top.
Comments: A very Piquant and gingery drink, suitable
for afternoon relaxation.

Iron Man

Ingredients
Glass: 350mL/12 oz Fancy Hi-Ball Glass
Mixers: 1 egg
           45mL/1½ oz Honey
           1 ripe Banana, sliced
           150mL/5 oz Orange juice

Method
Blend with ice and pour.

Garnish: A vanilla bean floated, then sprinkle flake chocolate over top.

Comments: Choc-a-block with energy.
Created by Rowan Sapwell, Manager, Fishermen's Pier Restaurant Geelong.

Island Paradise

Ingredients
Glass: 90mL/3 oz Martini Glass
Mixers: 30mL/1 oz Orange juice
           15mL/½ oz Coconut cream
           30mL/1 oz Lime juice
           dash Sugar syrup

Method
Shake with ice and strain.

Garnish: Lime slice and sprig of mint.

Comments: Tropical tastes in a short and piquant quencher.

Issy Wassy

Ingredients
Glass: 230mL/8 oz Hurricane Glass
Mixers: 125mL/4 oz Milk
                    $1/2$ Banana
                    2 slices Cantaloupe melon

Method
Blend with ice and pour.
Garnish: Cantaloupe slice with straws.
Comments: For the smooth stylish chap.

Jaffa

Ingredients
Glass: 200mL/6 oz Old Fashioned Glass
Mixers: scoop Chocolate Ice cream
                    90mL/3 oz Orange juice

Method
Blend with ice and pour.
Garnish: 1 teaspoon grated chocolate on top.
Comments: Just like a liquid jaffa.

Jersey Cow

Ingredients
Glass: 290mL/9 oz Old Fashioned Glass
Mixers: 180mL/6 oz Cola
               Scoop Chocolate Ice cream

Method
Stir over ice.
Garnish: Teaspoon of grated chocolate over top.
Comments: A choc-cola delight.

Jimmy's Beach Cruiser

Ingredients
Glass: 380mL/12 oz Viva Grande Glass
Mixers: 6 Raspberries
               2 tablespoons Crushed pineapple
               60mL/2 oz Orange juice
               Top-up with Lemonade (7-up)

Method
Blend with ice and pour.
Garnish: Two raspberries on side of glass, plus optional decoration.
Comments: A great blend of flavours.

Joh's Country

Ingredients

Glass: 350mL/12 oz Fiesta Grande Glass
Mixers: 45mL/1½ oz Pineapple juice
              30mL/1 oz Coconut cream
              dash Lime Cordial
              60mL/2 oz Mango and Orange juice

Method
Blend with ice and pour.
Garnish: mango slice, straw and optional decoration.
Comments: Rich creamy coconut flavour.

Juice Combo

Ingredients

Glass: 270mL/8 oz Footed Hi-Ball Glass
Mixers: 45mL/1½ oz Pineapple juice
              45mL/1½ oz Orange juice
              45mL/1½ oz Apple juice
              45mL/1½ oz Dark grape juice
              30mL/1 oz Lime juice
              15mL/½ oz Sugar syrup

Method
Build over ice and stir.
Garnish: Two dark table grapes on side of glass.
Comments: A refreshing blend of juices.

Julie's Black Cat

Ingredients

Glass: 270mL/9 oz Hi-Ball Glass
Mixers: 15mL/½ oz Lemon juice
              125mL/4 oz Dark grape juice
              60mL/2 oz Lemonade (7-up)
              60mL/2 oz Dry Ginger Ale

Method

Build over ice.

Garnish: Lemon twists dropped in glass, straw and optional decoration.

Comments: Let this one cross your path, a dry tasty drink.

Kate's Pink Echidna

Ingredients

Glass: 310mL/10 oz Hi-Ball Glass
Mixers: 3 Strawberries
              2 slices Cantaloupe Melon
              30mL/1 oz Sugar syrup
              dash Lemon juice
              Top-up with Lemonade (7-up)

Method

Blend with ice and pour.

Garnish: Cantaloupe slice and small strawberry on side of glass.

Comments: A delicate melon flavour.

Kerry's Rose Garden

Ingredients

Glass: 290mL/9 oz Salud Grande Glass
Mixers: 30mL/1 oz Dark grape juice
                1 tablespoon Watermelon
                15mL/¹/₂ oz Lemon juice
                ¹/₂ Egg white
                dash Sugar syrup

Method

Blend all ingredients except Cream, with ice and pour.
Garnish: Float cream, sprinkle with cinnamon.
Comments: A sharp drink, with subtle flavour.

Lavender

Ingredients

Glass: 210mL/7 oz Old Fashioned Glass
Mixers: 90mL/3 oz Dark grape juice
                15mL/¹/₂ oz Lemon juice
                15mL/¹/₂ oz Sugar syrup
                Top-up with Soda water

Method

Shake with ice and strain.
Garnish: Several red table grapes and lemon slice.
Comments: A lightly "grapesy" drink which is most refreshing before a meal.

Lazer Zap

Ingredients

Glass: 260mL/8 oz Margarita Glass
Mixers: 30mL/1 oz Lemon juice
                1 teaspoon Honey
                60mL/2 oz Grapefruit juice
                Top-up with Soda water

Method

Shake with ice and pour.

Garnish: Lemon slice, floated.

Comments: Grab your spacesuits, it will zap you out of this world.

Lemon Fizz

Ingredients

Glass: 260mL/8 oz Champagne Tulip Flute
Mixers: 180mL/5 oz Lemonade (7-up)
                30mL/1 oz Lemon juice
                scoop Lemon gelato

Method

Build over ice.

Garnish: Lemon slice and Italian flag.

Comments: A sweet lemon sensation.

Lethal Weapon

Ingredients
Glass: 310mL/10 oz Hi-Ball Glass
Mixers: 210mL/7 oz V8 juice
1 teaspoon Chilli sauce
salt and pepper
15mL/½ oz Lemon juice

Method
Build over ice and stir.
Garnish: Celery stalk.
Comments: Full of vitamins, but with a fiery bite at the end. A great heart starter at breakfast time.

Mangolite

Ingredients
Glass: 310mL/10 oz Hi-Ball Glass
Mixers: 150mL/5 oz Mango and Orange juice
60mL/2 oz Milk
dash Claytons Tonic
sachet Lite-n-Low

Method
Blend wit ice and pour.
Garnish: Optional decoration.
Comments: A smooth healthy drink.

Matt's Classic

Ingredients
Glass: 260mL/8 oz Tulip Champagne Flute
Mixers: 3 Strawberries
$^1/_2$ Kiwi fruit
60mL/2 oz Plain yoghurt
15mL/$^1/_2$ oz Sugar syrup

Method
Build with ice and pour.
Garnish: Kiwi slice on side of glass.
Comments: A thick fruity blend with a gentle hint of apricots.

Melon Delight

Ingredients
Glass: 270mL/8 oz Hi-Ball Glass
Mixers: 4 tablespoons Watermelon
2 tablespoons Canteloupe
2 tablespoons Honeydew melon
30mL/1 oz Lemon juice
2 teaspoons honey

Method
Blend with ice and pour.
Garnish: 1 ball of each of the melons.
Comments: A summer delight.
Created by Peter Podbury of Savvas Restaurant, Geelong.

Mickey Mouse

Ingredients
Glass: 270mL/8oz Hi-Ball Glass
Mixers: 90mL/3 oz Orange juice
            30mL/1 oz Raspberry cordial
            90mL/3 oz lemonade (7-up)

Method
Build over ice.
Garnish: Two cherries on side of glass.
Comments: A dash of vitamin C for you sweet tooth.

Milk Nog

Ingredients
Glass: 300mL/10 oz Footed Hi-Ball Glass
Mixers: 1 egg
            200mL/6 oz Milk
            30mL/1 oz Sugar syrup

Method
Shake with ice and pour.
Garnish: Vanilla bean, and a dusting of cinnamon.
Comments: Mother's favourite egg-flip for building healthy bodies.

Mintlup

Ingredients

Glass: 310mL/10 oz Hi-Ball Glass
Mixers: large sprig of crushed mint
15mL/¹/₂ oz Lime juice
90mL/3 oz Dry Ginger ale
90mL/3 oz Lemon & lime mineral water

Method

Build over ice.

Garnish: Mint leaf on lemon slice.

Comments: Southern hospitality in prohibition days perhaps.

Mocktini

Ingredients

Glass: 90mL/3 oz Martini Glass
Mixers: 15mL/¹/₂ oz Lime juice
dash Lemon juice
60mL/2 oz Tonic water

Method

Stir with ice and strain.

Garnish: A green olive on a toothpick or a lemon twist.

Comments: The classic cocktail, non-alcoholic version.

Mocquiri

Ingredients

Glass: 90mL/3 oz Martini Glass

Mixers: 60mL/2 oz Apple juice

15mL/½ oz Lemon juice

15mL/½ oz Sugar syrup

Method

Blend with Ice and strain

Garnish: Lemon or lime twist

Comments: An apple flavoured non-alcoholic Daiquiri.

Nick's Health Drink

Ingredients

Glass: 290mL/9 oz Poco Grande Glass

Mixers: 60mL/2 oz V8 juice

60mL/2 oz Orange juice

120mL/4 oz Natural yoghurt

Method

Shake with ice and strain.

Garnish: Carrot top and straw.

Comments: Very definely a healthy drink.

Oramato

Ingredients
Glass: 240mL/8 oz Footed Hi-Ball Glass
Mixers: 90mL/3 oz Tomato juice
              125mL/4 oz Orange juice

Method
Shake with Ice and Pour
Garnish: Orange peel curl.
Comments: Try this orange tomato for a taste difference.

Paradise Quencher

Ingredients
Glass: 310mL/10 oz Hi-Ball Glass
Mixers: $^1/_3$ small banana
              slice mango
              60mL/2 oz Orange and mango juice
              top-up with lemonade (7-up)

Method
Blend with ice and pour.
Garnish: Banana and mango slices on side of glass, serve with straws.
Comments: The sweet succulent flavours of tropical fruit.

Passionate

Ingredients

Glass: 230mL/7 oz Hurricane Glass
Mixers: 1 teaspoon passionfruit pulp
60mL/2 oz Grapefruit juice
dash lime juice
dash Grenadine
mineral water to top-up

Method

Blend with ice and pour.
Garnish: Lime slice on side of glass.
Comments: Wait for the after tang!

Peach Magic

Ingredients

Glass: 440mL/14 oz Hurricane Glass
Mixers: 1 Peach or Apricot, stoned
90mL/3 oz Orange and mango juice
90mL/3 oz Apple juice
top-up with Dry Ginger Ale

Method

Build over ice and pour.
Garnish: Watermelon slice and stemmed maraschino cherry.
Comments: A large refreshing taste of the orchard.

Peninsula Pelican

Ingredients

Glass: 290mL/9 oz Old Fashioned Glass

Mixers: 90mL/3 oz Apple juice

                  1/2 Egg white

                  2 teaspoons honey

Method

Blend with ice and pour.

Garnish: Straws and optional decoration.

Comments: Sweet treat before that moonlight stroll.

Pina Con Nada

Ingredients

Glass: 270mL/9 oz Footed Hi-Ball Glass

Mixers: 90mL/3 oz Pineapple juice

                  30mL/1 oz Coconut cream

                  15mL/1/2 oz Sugar syrup

Method

Blend with ice and pour.

Garnish: Wedge of pineapple and a strawberry with straws.

Comments: The creamy non-alcoholic version of the famous Pina Colada.

Pink Froth

Ingredients
Glass: 490mL/16 oz Fiesta Grande Glass
Mixers: 60mL/2 oz Cream
45mL/1½ oz Sugar syrup
15mL/½ oz Grenadine
15mL/½ oz Lemon juice
15mL/½ oz Lime juice
top-up with lemonade (7-up)

Method
Blend with ice and pour.
Garnish: Optional decoration.
Comments: Sweet creamy and smooooooth.

Queensland Crush

Ingredients
Glass: 270mL/8 oz Hi-Ball Glass
Mixers: 150mL/5 oz Orange juice
3 tablespoons crushed pineapple
15mL/½ oz Lemon juice
15mL/½ oz Sugar syrup

Method
Blend with ice and pour.
Garnish: Pineapple wedge, orange slice.
Comments: A tropical refresher.

Quenchie

Ingredients
Glass: 390mL/13 oz Poco Grande Glass
Mixers: 150mL/5 oz Orange juice
               150mL/5 oz Lemonade (7-up)
               2 dessertspoons passionfruit pulp

Method
Build over ice and stir.
Garnish: Slice of orange, slice of lemon with 2 marachino cherries on toothpicks, serve with swizzle sticks and straws.
Comments: Created by Maxine Nash of Bubbles-Wodonga
Hotel, was runner-up in the Best Border Beverage Competition.

Red Magic

Ingredients
Glass: 140mL/5 oz Cocktail Glass
Mixers: 90mL/3 oz Apple juice
               4 Raspberries
               1 teaspoon honey

Method
Blend with ice and strain.
Garnish: Raspberries on side of glass, with a little mint.
Comments: You will "bee" pleasantly surprised.

Shirley Temple

Ingredients

Glass: 310mL/10 oz Hi-Ball Glass
Mixers: 15mL/½ oz Grenadine
ginger ale or lemonade (7-up) to top-up

Method

Build over ice.
Garnish: Slice of orange, serve with swizzle stick and two straws.
Comments: For a tangy variation to this drink try a Shirley Temple No.2. Use the following: 60ml pineapple juice to a glass half full of ice. Top with lemonade (7-up), float 15mL/½ oz passionfruit pulp on top and garnish with pineapple wedge and cherry.

Shrinking Violet

Ingredients

Glass: 270mL/9 oz Hi-Ball Glass
Mixers: 125mL/4 oz Dark Grape juice
90mL/3 oz Lemonade (7-up)
15mL/½ oz Lime juice

Method

Build with ice and stir.
Garnish: Two dark grapes and straw.
Comments: A light but sharp drink.

Silver Queen

Ingredients

Glass: 170mL/6 oz Tulip Champagne Flute
Mixers: 90mL/3 oz Sparkling White Grape juice
scoop Vanilla Ice cream

Method

Build over ice.

Garnish: Several white table grapes.

Comments: A wine spider (non-alcoholic of course)

Spazz

Ingredients

Glass: 310mL/10 oz Hi-Ball Glass
Mixers: $1/2$ Peach or Apricot, stoned
150mL/5 oz Pineapple juice
15mL/$1/2$ oz Lime juice

Method

Blend with ice and pour.

Garnish: Pour a teaspoon Grenadine over top of drink, add apricot slice and straw.

Comments: A long, delicately flavoured drink.

Strawberry Spider

Ingredients
Glass: 300mL/10 oz Footed Hi-Ball Glass
Mixers: 6 small strawberries
15mL/½ oz sugar syrup
90mL/3 oz Lemonade (7-up)
scoop strawberry ice cream

Method
Blend with ice all ingredients except lemonade (7-up) and ice cream.
Garnish: Pour blended ingredients in glass, almost fill with lemonade (7-up), then top-up with strawberry ice cream.
Place small whole strawberry on side.
Comments: Children's favourite.

Strawberry Zappie

Ingredients
Glass: 310mL/10 oz Hi-Ball Glass
Mixers: 4 strawberries
180mL/6 oz Apple juice
30mL/1 oz lemon juice
dash lime cordial

Method
Blend with ice and pour.
Garnish: Small strawberry on straw.
Comments: A sharp, tasty, refresher.

Sunburnt Kiwi

Ingredients

Glass: 440mL/14 oz Hurricane Glass

Mixers: 1 ripe plum, stoned
1 Kiwi fruit, skinned
15mL/1/2 oz Lemon juice
60mL/2 oz Dark grape juice
top-up with lemonade (7-up)

Method

Blend with ice and pour.

Garnish: Slice of kiwi fruit on side of glass.

Comments: A thick, rich drink from New Zealand.

Sundowner

Ingredients

Glass: 210mL/7 oz Old Fashion Glass

Mixers: 75mL/2 1/2 oz Orange Juice and mango juice
15mL/1/2 oz Lemon juice
45mL/1 1/2 oz Clayton's Tonic

Method

Shake with ice and pour.

Garnish: Lemon slice, floated

Comment: A citrus tang to activate the taste buds.

Sunshine

Ingredients
Glass: 270mL/9 oz Hi-Ball Glass
Mixers: 90mL/3 oz Pineapple juice
                30mL/1 oz Coconut cream
                ½ Banana
                30mL/1 oz Cream
                30mL/1 oz Sugar syrup

Method
Blend with ice and pour.

Garnish: Wedge of pineapple and one cherry. Serve with swizzle stick and straw.

Comments: Created by Maxine Nash of Bubbles-Wodonga Hotel, was a runner-up in Best Border Beverage Competition.

Surf Coast Sunset

Ingredients
Glass: 200mL/6 oz Old Fashioned Glass
Mixers: 60mL/2 oz Apple juice
                60mL/2 oz Orange juice
                ¹/₂ teaspoon Grenadine

Method
Build over ice and stir.

Garnish: Orange slice with cherry in the centre.

Comments: Add the Grenadine last and watch it sink to the bottom as the setting sun.

Sydneysider

Ingredients

Glass: 350mL/12 oz Fiesta Grande Glass
Mixers: 30mL/1 oz Lemon juice
30mL/1 oz Orange juice
30mL/1 oz Grapefruit juice
30mL/1 oz Pineapple juice
60mL/2 oz Apple juice
½ Egg white
dash Grenadine

Method

Shake with ice and pour.
Garnish: Apple fan.
Comments: Fruit medley in the Opera House.
Created by Anthony Carroll of The Fresh Ketch Restaurant.

Tassie Shot

Ingredients

Glass: 200mL/6 oz Old Fashioned Glass
Mixers: 125mL/4 oz Apple juice
60mL/2 oz Grapefruit juice
1 sachet Lite-n-low

Method

Shake with ice and pour
Garnish: Straw through slice of apple on top.
Comments: The apple of your eye.

Tropical Rain

Ingredients
Glass: 330mL/11 oz Hi-Ball Glass
Mixers: tablespoon passionfruit pulp
125mL/4 oz Pineapple juice
$^1/_2$ ripe Mango
30mL/1 oz Plain yoghurt
dash Grenadine

Method
Blend with ice and pour..

Garnish: Mango slices and raspberry on toothpick on side of glass.

Comments: A thick tropical drink, with the tarty flavour of passionfruit.

Virgin Maria

Ingredients
Glass: 270mL/8 oz Footed Hi-Ball Glass
Mixers: 180mL/6 oz Tomato juice
dash Lemon juice
15mL/$^1/_2$ oz chilli sauce

Method
Blend with ice and pour.

Garnish: Cucumber slice, cherry tomatoes and optional decoration.

Comments: A very hot and spicy drink, guaranteed to keep you that way.

Virgin Mary

Ingredients

Glass: 270mL/8 oz Hi-Ball Glass
Mixers: 150mL/5 oz Tomato juice
15mL/1/2 oz Lemon juice
teaspoon Worcestershire sauce
2 or 3 drops Tabasco sauce
Salt and pepper to taste

Method

Build over ice and stir.
Garnish: Celery stalk, lemon slice and straws.
Comments: A spicy refreshing start to the day.

Wallington Special

Ingredients

Glass: 270mL/8 oz Footed Hi-Ball Glass
Mixers: 6 Strawberries
180mL/6 oz Pineapple juice
1/2 Egg white
15mL/1/2 oz Sugar syrup

Method

Blend with ice and pour.
Garnish: Small strawberry on side of glass and straw.
Comments: Tropical fruity blend.

West Coast Splash

Ingredients

Glass: 290mL/9 oz Salud Grande Glass

Mixers: 6 mint leaves

60mL/2 oz Orange and Mango juice

top-up with Dry Ginger Ale

Method

Shake with ice and pour.

Garnish: Mint leaves, plus optional decoration.

Comments: This drink will certainly "dry" you off.

Witch's Kiss

Ingredients

Glass: 330mL/11 oz Hi-Ball Glass

Mixers: 150mL/5 oz Tropical Fruit Juice

dash Lemon juice

dash Sugar syrup

15mL/1/2 oz Grenadine

top-up with soda water

Method

Shake with ice and pour.

Garnish: Lemon slice on side of glass, serve with straws and optional decoration.

Comments: A light tropical flavour.

Cocktail index

Shooters index

Non-alcoholic index